THE GOD OF TOMORROW:

WHITEHEAD AND TEILHARD ON METAPHYSICS, MYSTICISM, AND MISSION

BRUCE G. EPPERLY

Energion Publications
Cantonment, Florida
2024

Scripture quotations are paraphrased by the author.

Cover Design: Henry E. Neufeld

ISBN: 978-1-63199-895-9
eISBN: 978-1-63199-896-6
Library of Congress Control Number: 2024935785

Energion Publications
1241 Conference Rd
Cantonment, FL 32533

energion.com
pubs@energion.com

TABLE OF CONTENTS

For some time now the principal interest of my life is no longer Fossil Man, but the Man of Tomorrow; or, more exactly, the "God of tomorrow," since I am more and more convinced that the great event of our time is a kind of change in the face of God.[1]

[God] does not create the world, [God] saves it: or more accurately, [God] is the poet of the world with tender patience leading it by [his] vision of truth, beauty, and goodness.[2]

1 "Letter to Idea Treat," August 30, 1950. Quoted in Ursula King, *Spirit of Fire: The Life and Vision of Teilhard de Chardin* (Maryknoll, NY: Orbis Books, 2015), 204.

2 Alfred North Whitehead, *Process and Reality: Corrected Edition* (New York: Free Press, 1979), 346

BEGINNINGS:
A CALL TO
THEOLOGICAL ADVENTURE

Religion will not regain its old power until it can face change in the same spirit as does science. Its principles may be eternal, but the expression of those principles requires continual development. This evolution of religion is in the main a disengagement of its own proper ideas from the adventitious notions which have crept into it by reason of the expression of its own ideas in terms of the imaginative picture of the world entertained in previous ages.[1]

The world must have a God; but our concept of God must be extended as the dimensions of our world are extended.[2]

"Be not conformed to this age but be transformed by the renewing of your mind!" so counseled the Apostle Paul (Romans 12:2). God is on the move and so is the world: be ready to change your mind, transform your vision of the universe, and become a new creation. Imagine new visions of God and the universe and awaken to God in the smallest speck and the grandest galaxy. Prepare for a cosmic adventure, a roller coaster ride from the Big Bang to Artificial Intelligence and Beyond. You are part of a Holy

---

1   Alfred North Whitehead, *Science and the Modern World* (New York: Free Press, 1967), 189.
2   Pierre Teilhard de Chardin, "Letters from a Traveler." Quoted in Ursula King, *Spirit Fire: The Life and Vision of Teilhard de Chardin* (Maryknoll, NY: Orbis Books, 2015), 58.

Adventure, and how you respond to the call of adventure will sow the seeds of creative transformation or the plotlines of planetary destruction. Remember that as bold as your imagined adventures are, they can never exceed God's imagination for you and the universe. This was the message of the Apostle Paul in the first century and the call to theological, scientific, and philosophical adventures in our time. Be not conformed to the past, but open to God of Tomorrow's invitation to future creative transformation.

In your wildest wonderings and wanderings, you will discover that you are not alone. There is an Adventurer moving through this universe – and every other universe – from the very beginning, inspiring, enlightening, enlivening, energizing, and inviting you to say "yes" to adventures to come. "Not all who wander are lost," so says J.R.R. Tolkien, and we are not lost in the cosmos, when we travel with the Holy Adventurer as our companion. We are comrades on a pilgrimage of Holy Evolution and our religious world views must evolve and expand to be faithful to the Christ of the Cosmos.

Over twenty-five-hundred years ago, the poet who wrote Psalm 8 marveled at the universe and its Creator and then asked a provocative question: "When I look at your heavens, the work of your fingers; the moon and the stars you have established, what are human beings that you are mindful of them, mortals that your care for them?" Gazing at the starry skies and pondering the immense intergalactic journey, we exclaim with the same spirit, "How great thou art" in praise of the Creative Wisdom that brings forth the universe day by day.

Yet, we also confess as we look at images from the Hubble and Webb telescopes, "Do we really matter in the vastness of the universe?" We are humbled as residents of the tiny speck we call home, whirling about an average star, in a solar system, just one of over a trillion planets in our galaxy, hurtling among two trillion galaxies in the observable universe. We appear to be nothing, and our lives are the equivalent of but a few seconds in the immense cosmic and planetary journey. We wonder with the Psalmist,

"Why would we be chosen to be companions in a Holy Adventure of cosmos creation?" And, yet, we have a vocation that is ours alone on planet Earth: "you [God] have made humans a little lower than God, and crowned them with glory and honor. You have given them dominion over the works of your hands." (Psalm 8:3-6a) We are, as Robert Frost said of a mite running across a white sheet of paper, "a considerable speck" and yet we journey with God and all creation.

We are awestruck at the immensity and age of the universe. We also know that in some mysterious way, the creative energy of the universe flows in and through us, giving us life and purpose. We are the children of the Big Bang and evolving universe, who have the ability to marvel and praise and then shape the planet upon which we live. Barely noticeable in the universe that dwarfs our imaginations, we have a vocation to guide our planet's journey, repair the damage done by prior generations and our own, and become healers of our planet's future. To the spiritual seeker, there is an omnipresent God or Wise Energy that centers us, valuing us in a world of countless other centers of value. God has the trillion-galaxy "whole world in God's hands" and also, "you and me brother, and you and me sister," as the spiritual chants.[3]

Change and Conflict in Science and Theology. The religious journey involves the contrast of the cosmic and the personal, the infinite and the finite, and the one and the many. These contrasts have inspired mystic awe and wonder and philosophical adventure and also the small spirited desire to control history and the human imagination. Immensity can inspire spiritual and scientific adventure; it can also provoke reducing the scope of our world and religious world view to manageable bites and limiting the infinite God to easily recited and required formulae, whose adherence is necessary to achieve eternal life. Not everyone wants to embark on a Holy Adventure. Not everyone or every institution wants to jettison familiar pathways for uncertain horizons. Some institutions yearn for the good old days, fearing that change will threaten

---

3   "He's Got the Whole World in His Hands," African American Spiritual.

their privileged place in God's affections and in determining the priorities of the nation and planet.

Change is unavoidable, but it is also overwhelming. Change means we must embrace the God of Tomorrow. We must let go of cherished understandings of God and ourselves, not to mention our understanding of economics, politics, international relations, and ecology, to be faithful to God's vision in our time and place. We may even have to revise our understandings of God, Christ, church, revelation, human possibility, science, and salvation, jettisoning or deemphasizing beloved traditions to be faithful to God's new creation. That takes imagination, courage, and hope in the future. It may even require hope in the God of Tomorrow, trusting that God may be the source as well as inspiration of the changes with which we struggle.

For two thousand years, the most insightful Christian leaders have sought to deal with changing visions of the universe and our planet. They have struggled to understand our place in the context of the infinite and finite, and diversity and otherness, and have constructed spiritually sound ways to join order and novelty, whether in theology, science, culture, literature, or the world religions. Amazed by the wonders of God's love in creation, they have sought to be humble pilgrims on an immense journey with their Creator and their fellow creatures. Novelty and diversity inspired their imagination and expanded their understanding of the Divine. God is always more than we can imagine and so is the universe, our planet, and human existence.

In contrast to these intrepid adventures of the spirit, other Christian leaders, terrified by visions of God's grandeur, substituted rigid and static dogma for Divine Mystery. No doubt, they were well intentioned. In their minds, our eternal salvation is at stake. If we jettison the old ways, what will be left? If we get it wrong, will we forfeit eternal beatitude with God? If we question dogma, authority, scripture, and sacrament, we may be forced to question our images of God and the saving love of Jesus. For champions of orthodox doctrine and authoritarian institutional-

ism, change, diversity, and mystery, threaten the unchanging doctrines and practices of their "one, true church, delivered by Jesus
to the saints."

To protect their faith and their right to control the keys to
God's kingdom, religious authorities, often bolstered by the support of political leaders, silence, then and now, theological, political, and scientific change agents and those who revel in the deep
mysteries of existence. A small and controllable god and an equally
small and controllable Christ, both of whom stood for the status quo, are seen as Christianity's safeguard against the relativism
fostered by scientific discovery, medical advance, pluralism, and
social change.

One of the old standbys of the Baptist church of my childhood celebrated unchanging faith in a sea of relativism. I can
still hear the lyrics that gave the faithful confidence to stand firm
against the perils of science and pluralism.

> Give me that old time religion,
> Give me that old time religion,
> Give me that old time religion,
> It's good enough for me.

> It was good for my mother,
> It was good for my father,
> It was good for my mother,
> It's good enough for me.

But, is the old-time religion truly good enough for us today?
Is the old-time religion simply "old" and no longer agile enough
to respond to a lively universe? Does holding onto the old-time
religion, its doctrines of the young earth, three-story universe,
original sin, and conflict of faith and science, prevent us from
responding to the challenges of our time and embracing our vocation in an uncertain world? Similar in spirit to their Protestant

and Catholic predecessors, the Baptists of my childhood sought
a faith that was secure, strong, and self-contained, fully aligned
with a literal understanding of the words of their black-backed
Bibles. New insights found in science and literature were potential threats to those who sought to hold onto past understandings
of God and the world. When my undergraduate professor and
mentor, Professor Marie Fox received her Ph.D. in Philosophy at
Cornell University, a local pastor in the West Virginia coal town
from which she hailed preached about the perils of higher education. To that small town preacher and many of the Christians of
my childhood, the Bible was the word of God, explaining every
aspect of life from science to sexuality, and persons had to choose
between a literal understanding of God's word and the vicissitudes
of human speculation. New ideas threatened the old-time religion
and the social structures and privilege it supported. When our
elders chanted "God is the same yesterday, today, and tomorrow,"
they meant that believers could discover the truths of science and
ethics simply by consulting their bibles and studying the six-day
creation and fall story, described in the first three chapters of Genesis. If science and scripture disagreed, the faithful have only one
choice: to trust God's infallible revelation in scripture and eccle-
siastic tradition and abandon the temptations of the world, flesh,
and devil, embodied in the theory of evolution, the emerging
understandings of psychology and sexuality, and encounters with
non-Christian religious traditions.

Still, the forces of change and growth in religion and society
continue to move forward. Since my childhood in the 1950s, the
world has changed radically and so has my theological vision. The
moral, scientific, and spiritual arcs of history and planetary life
cannot be defeated by book banning or teaching intelligent design
and the young earth or humans walking around with dinosaurs as
legitimate science in public schools. In contrast to those who hold
onto the **God of Yesterday**, I believe that the future of Christianity, and the future of the nation and planet, depend on our wise
embrace of the forces of movement, change, and transformation

in science, technology, spirituality, human rights, and climatology. Our hope to meet the challenges of the future can be inspired only by a **God of Tomorrow**, whose wise creativity enables us to meet the technologies and changes of the future with wisdom and compassion. Yesterday's God cannot be entirely jettisoned. We must honor the insights and piety of those who came before us. But the **God of Tomorrow** calls us beyond established orders to new possibilities and challenges us to join the gifts of the past with the hopes and novelties of the future.

A Way Forward in the Adventure of Science and Religion. There is another path for people of faith, the path of the constantly renewed mind, grounded in the vision of dynamic and open-spirited divinity who delights in change and evolution and supports a partnership of faith and science. There is a path that embraces love of the Earth and commitment to spiritual growth. There is an adventurous way forward in which science can be a friend of faith, and not the enemy perceived by orthodox Christians and materialist scientists. There is faith come of age with a God and spirituality as large as the universe and as spacious as the diversity of our own planet. There are world-shaping pioneers on this path who are willing to embark on adventures of ideas, theological reflection, ecclesiastical transformation, and spiritual practice as bold as the universe in which we live.

This text describes the impact of two theological and scientific pioneers in expanding our vision of Christianity and the relationship of religion and science, Alfred North Whitehead and Pierre Teilhard de Chardin. Their work provides a way for seekers and active Christians alike to love God with their minds as well as their hearts. The way of Teilhard and Whitehead provides a vision for a Christ for the Cosmos and a Divine Companion in the Holy Adventure of planetary and cosmic evolution.

Philosopher Alfred North Whitehead asserts that the process is the reality. All things flow and God is found in the maelstrom of history as the source of both novelty and order, and on occasion the conflict of static doctrines with new visions of humanity and its cosmic environment. What appears to be chaos may be the birth of a new understanding of humankind or even the birth of a new galaxy! The unyielding conservative, whether in ethics, science, culture, or religion goes against the grain of the universe, according to Whitehead. There are no absolute and unchanging certainties, nor can we ensure that God will rescue us and our planet from our own foolishness. An evolutionary world is also amazing and inspiring and at times threatening to those who bravely sail forth on the high seas of adventure. Still, despite the challenges, God lures us forward toward new horizons of faith, science, and spirituality with God's vision of truth, beauty, and goodness.

For these intellectual and spiritual adventurers, the universe is alive and on the move and so is their vision of God. The priest-scientist Pierre Teilhard de Chardin proclaims a universe on fire with loving energy, leaning forward from the humble beginnings of single celled organisms toward fulfillment in the realization of a global spiritual consciousness, inspired by Christ the Evolver.

As pilgrims of the future, to use Teilhard's self-description, Whitehead and Teilhard charted a forward-looking theological and cosmological vision that inspires an adventurous faith. Faith lives by what it affirms, not what it denies, and a living faith affirms that God is faithful and that God's fidelity is revealed in God's novel and transformative presence in the orderly movements of the seasons, the insights of prophets, mystics, and scientists and, in the immense creative advances of evolution. Faithful in the past, God is the source of hope in the future, as the inspiration to change and growth.

As we face the future, we need to be bold spiritually and institutionally. New adventures inspire further adventures, novel discoveries open the door to new possibilities and the doors of perception are flung wide to reveal a sacred universe, guided by an intimate and personal Wisdom. Humankind is not fixed or finished in its evolution and exploration. We cannot afford to be passive, trusting everything to the machinations of either an omnipotent God or rapidly emerging technological and informational advances. We need a vision of God that responds to our expanding visions of the universe and provides inspiration to face a rapidly changing, and often frightening, world. I believe that we will find such a vision in the theological and scientific adventures of Whitehead and Teilhard.

Adventure inspires intellectual and spiritual growth and the realization that the horizons toward which we are beckoned can never be fully encompassed by human religious, scientific, and cultural constructs. Time-worn doctrines of a parochial Jesus, a datable moment of original sin by the primordial couple Adam and Eve, and Christian exclusiveness are too cramped to provide guidance, inspiration, and hope for humankind. We need a Christ for the Cosmos, a still evolving Christ, and, as Ilia Delio proclaims, a "Not-Yet God," whose presence inspires our commitment to the planet and our non-human companions. We need a vision of God large enough and yet intimate enough to challenge us to claim our vocation as earth keepers and earth healers. God is still speaking in our hearts and in the urge for further planetary and cosmic adventure, and for an expansive vision of humankind and a healing technology.

As our understanding of God, the universe, and human and non-human evolution continues to grow, we need guideposts for the human adventure in science, economics, technology, and spirituality. In our evolving and processive world, I believe that we can find inspiration, challenge, and guidance for the journey from two fellow adventurers, Alfred North Whitehead and Pierre Teilhard de Chardin. Independent of one another in forming their visions of the universe, Whitehead and Teilhard charted a vision of the universe large enough to embrace both the science and religion of today and also tomorrow.[4] Committed to pursuing truth wherever

---

4 There is evidence from Teilhard's correspondence that he knew of
   Whitehead's work and was impressed by Whitehead's image of adventure
   in science and religion. Though not directly influenced by Whitehead's
   metaphysical vision, Teilhard may have seen Whitehead as a kindred spirit

it led, whether in laboratory, fossil field, observatory, classroom, or sanctuary, they saw religious experience as life-transforming precisely because of its openness to growth and change.

Based on their uncompromising commitment to integrating theology and science, Whitehead and Teilhard challenged static and backward-looking doctrines that substitute abstractions for encounters with the Living God, moving through history, science, and culture. They recognized that dogmatic formulas leave in their wake religious institutions that are irrelevant to the world in which we live. Whitehead counseled that:

> Religion will not regain its old power until it can face change in the same spirit as does science. Its principles may be eternal, but the expression of those principles requires continual development.[5]

Clashes between visions of reality, doctrinal positions, and prior understandings of the relationship of science and religion open the doors for new visions of faith. Whitehead believed that discord in science and religion may foreshadow the emergence of vital spirituality and social transformation.

In similar fashion, Teilhard asserted that the Roman Catholic leadership's attachment to intellectually indefensible doctrines such as the original sin of Adam and Eve stifled the movements of God's Spirit in the church and rendered the doctrines of Roman Catholicism and its Protestant siblings unbelievable to twentieth century persons. Science and faith, and most particularly the theory of evolution, can support one another and provide moral and spiritual resources for seekers within and beyond our churches. Teilhard believed that a living and relevant faith needed to be saved from religious authorities, who force people to choose between faith and science, and heaven and earth.

---

in the quest for a god large enough to embrace the findings of physics, biology, and evolutionary science.

5   Alfred North Whitehead, *Science and the Modern World,* (New York: Free Press, 1997), 189.

While both Whitehead and Teilhard had a keen appreciation for history and tradition, they recognized that fidelity to yesterday's insights and inspirations should not imprison us in the past but call us forward toward novel understandings of faith and science, and their relationship in companionship with a forward moving God. This is not just a matter of human choice but divine invitation; God is the source of the call forward. God lures the universe, part and whole toward new spiritual and scientific possibilities. Indeed, in the history of Christianity, saints and mystics, like scientists, were innovators in their time, whose orthodoxy was often questioned by the proponents of spiritual and institutional stasis.

Religion is a "adventure of the spirit," as Whitehead notes, inviting us to venture toward new horizons of faith and practice. "Hold fast to adventure," Teilhard counsels. Adventure gives zest to religion and breathes new life into the spiritual journey. To flourish, our religious traditions and theological perspectives need breathing space and an open future. We need to privilege novelty as well as order, and innovation as well as tradition. We need to see God as a fellow adventurer, calling us to be adventurous theologically, spirituality, and ethically. We also need a flexible theological and spiritual GPS for the journey ahead, knowing the future is uncertain, risky, and yet exciting.

In the quest to provide guidance and inspiration as we ponder the movements of evolution and the dangers of our time, this text explores the adventures of theological ideas, spiritual formation, and human responsibility and vocation from the perspective of Alfred North Whitehead and Pierre Teilhard de Chardin. It is my belief that these organic and holistic thinkers and spiritual guides provide a pathway to joining metaphysics (our vision of the universe and our place in it), mysticism (transformative encounters with the Holy), and mission (our vocation in an exciting and uncertain universe). In dialoguing with these two innovative thinkers, and adapting their wisdom for our age, we can frame a credible vision of reality, grounded in the dynamic interplay of mind, body, spirit, and social responsibility, integrating spirituality, social justice, cosmology, and science.

The task ahead is ultimately "theo-spiritual" in nature. It involves the interplay of an expansive theological vision, the promise that we can experience our deeply held theological visions, and practices that enable us to live fully and faithfully as global and cosmic citizens. Spirituality grounds and gives life to our theological perspectives and theological reflection provides intellectual grounding for our spiritual experiences. A loosely held "theo-spirituality" also invites scientists to consider the values and purposes inherent in the universe and the scientific adventure. To illuminate and incarnate the organic partnership of theology, spirituality, and science affirmed by Whitehead and Teilhard, I conclude each chapter with spiritual practices. Spirituality, theology, and science have unique gifts with which to enrich one another, while still preserving the integrity of the search for truth appropriate to each discipline.

A Personal Word. In the course of this project, I reread my dogeared and battered copy of the *Phenomenon of Man,* now best translated as the *Human Phenomenon,* and was transported back to 1973, when I purchased the book to augment my readings in a class on "Process Theology" at San Jose State University, taught by Richard Keady, a former Roman Catholic priest and recent Ph.D. from Claremont Graduate School. While the primary orientation of the class was Whiteheadian process theology, I found the evolutionary theology of Teilhard de Chardin captivating and congruent with Whitehead's metaphysical vision. During the final year of US involvement in the Vietnam War, I discovered that Teilhard presented a vision of hope that complemented Whitehead's affirmative cosmology as well as the idealism of the "summers of love" that had promised the dawning of the Age of Aquarius. In those days of national chaos, not unlike our time today, we could imagine a better future, and then set about building a new world in which technology and politics served humankind and the planet.

The Evolving God wanted – and needed – us to play our role in healing and evolving the earth!

In Whitehead and Teilhard, I found a creative and inspirational alternative to the conservative theological doctrines of my Baptist childhood. I found a God to believe in and a faith to affirm. I experienced, first, intellectually, and then spiritually, a Christ for the cosmos. I discovered a theological undergirding for my emerging spirituality, involvement in social and environmental justice, and affirmation of religious pluralism.

While for over fifty years most of my theological reflections have been influenced by the Whiteheadian stream of process theology, I have recently reclaimed the wisdom of Teilhard's process theology. This text marks one of the first attempts at a creative synthesis of Whitehead and Teilhard to birth a more holistic vision of process theology, if not the first attempt in a full-length book. More than ever, I am certain that we need to update our vision of God and the world to respond positively to global climate change, economic injustice, violations of human rights, and authoritarian politics and religion. Faith flourishes by its affirmations and not its negations and the world of Whitehead and Teilhard foster the "affirmative mysticism," as Quaker mystic Rufus Jones counsels, an Earth oriented and socially responsible theology enabling us to be faithful to God and God's creation "for just such a time as this."

This text follows an unfolding pattern. In the course of my reflections, I will, first, place the insights of Whitehead and Teilhard in the context of the religious, cultural, and scientific challenges of our time, and in certain cases relate them to my own theological and spiritual journey. Then, I will outline a Whiteheadian and Teilhardian approach to metaphysics, mysticism, and mission. I will explore ways that Whitehead and Teilhard can illuminate our twenty-first century religious and cultural challenges. In the course of this text, I will respond to issues that, given their historical context, were peripheral to their writings: ecology, religious pluralism, and racial justice. Finally, I will attempt a brief creative synthesis related to Whitehead's and Teilhard's metaphysics, mysticism, and mission, noting their common ground as an inspiration for our time and conclude with spiritual practices to awaken us the presence of the Holy Adventure coursing through our lives. I recognize that as one who has studied and sought to live by the theological vision articulated by Whitehead and Teilhard in my understanding of Christianity and the spiritual life, there will be places in this text where my voice and theirs will be in full alignment and I will be speaking for them as well as myself. While I seek to be faithful to their vision, I also realize that now as a mature theologian and spiritual guide who has sought to "live" process theology for fifty years, I also reflect intimately this vision in mind, body, spirit, and politics.

A Word of Thanks. Ubuntu, "I am because of you. We are because of each other," is a fundamental affirmation undergirding my personal theology and my reflections on Teilhard and Whitehead. This book is the fruitage of a lifetime of relationships with remarkable people in the give and take of theological reflection and spiritual and professional formation. I am grateful to my theological mentors John Cobb, Bernard Loomer, and David Griffin, and to my undergraduate professors Richard Keady and Marie Fox, who first introduced me to process theology. I am ever thankful to Rev. John Akers, my pastor at Grace Baptist Church in San Jose, California, whose quest for a living theology inspired him to join me in my first process theology course, in 1973, and who saw a theologian in a long-haired hippie college student.

For nearly fifty years, Jay McDaniel and Catherine Keller have been intellectual and spiritual companions, initially through our studies at Claremont Graduate School and since that time as artists and creators of the evolving process theology and spirituality through their teaching and writing. On a more personal note, I am grateful to Catherine Keller who was "matchmaker" to my wife Kate and I in the Fall of 1977. I can still remember Catherine reading Gerard Manley Hopkins' process-oriented "Pied Beauty" and "God's Grandeur" at our wedding in January 1979. Without Kate's companionship, I would not be the theologian I am today.

I am thankful for the efforts of my editor Chris Eyre and publisher Henry Neufeld, who encouraged me to think big and make great thoughts relevant to everyday life.

I am grateful to the creativity and energy of Ilia Delio and my Georgetown University colleague for two decades, Jack Haught for reigniting my interest in Teilhard and their giving life and motion to Teilhard's theological vision. The Center for Christogenesis' and Center for Process Studies' sponsorship of a conference on Whitehead and Teilhard inspired me to try my hand at a creative synthesis of these adventurous thinkers. I dedicate this text to Delio and Haught and pray that the impact of their work expands to encompass wider and wider circles of creative transformation.

This book is also dedicated to my grandchildren Jack and James, and their generation of children and those who follow them. May they experience the God of Tomorrow in a world which leans toward truth, beauty, goodness, and healing. May they live in the hopeful, peaceable, and creative realm envisaged by Whitehead and Teilhard. And, in the spirit of Teilhard, Whitehead, and the theo-spiritual evolutionary adventure, let us surround our reflections and study with prayer.

> *We thank you, evolving and creating God,*
> *for the wonder of all being.*
> *For illuminated minds and adventurous spirits.*
> *For the insights of Alfred North Whitehead*
> *and Pierre Teilhard de Chardin*
> *And for adventurers in the interplay of scientific discovery*
> *and theological reflection.*
> *We ask for courage to explore new visions*
> *and challenge outdated doctrines.*
> *And for appreciation of the beauty of the*
> *earth and the splendor of the skies.*
> *Inspire us to be your in companions*
> *in building the earth,*
> *Healing the nations,*

Moving from self-interest to world loyalty,
And separation to unity of spirit.
Bless our ever-expanding understanding of your universe
And Bless our quest to know, love, and care for the planet
And our human and non-human companions
    on this Good Earth. Amen.

1

The Measure of the Men: A Tale of Two Adventurers

The worship of God is not a rule of safety — it is an adventure of the spirit, a flight after the unattainable. The death of religion comes with the repression of the high hope of adventure.[1]

For some time now the principal interest of my life is no longer Fossil Man, but the Man of Tomorrow; or, more exactly, the God of Tomorrow, since I am more and more convinced that the great event of our time is a kind of change in the face of God.[2]

Imagine that religion is an adventure of the spirit in quest of the God of Tomorrow! Visualize a religion that encourages intellectual and spiritual restlessness as well as comfort. That promotes questions as well as answers, and novelty as well as familiarity. Our great religious traditions were inspired by adventurous quests. Think of Buddha's quest for enlightenment, Amos' prophetic challenge of injustice, Socrates' questioning of the gods of Athens, and Mother (Saint) Teresa's mission to the marginalized and forgotten. Think of Mary of Nazareth's "yes" to the angelic visitation and Mary of Magdala's presentation of the good news of resurrection

---

1   Alfred North Whitehead, *Science and the Modern World,* 192.

2   "Letter to Idea Treat," August 30, 1950. Quoted in Ursula King, *Spirit of Fire: The Life and Vision of Teilhard de Chardin* (Maryknoll, NY: Orbis Books, 2015), 204.

to Jesus' frightened male followers. That same adventurous spirit is what you have in the intellectual and spiritual journeys of Whitehead and Teilhard.

Alfred North Whitehead proclaims that the world lives by the incarnation of God. God's incarnation transforms the present age in light of God's vision of the future. God's presence in the world is global and also personal. Whitehead asserts that on a global level the "teleology of the universe is aimed at the production of beauty."[3] God has a long-term vision for the cosmos, planet earth, humankind, and each individual. This same vision energizes and is partially incarnate in each and every occasion of experience. The moral and spiritual arcs of the universe and history inspire each person and every moment of experience and call us to adventure and growth, individually and nationally. Divinity influences the direction of our freedom and creativity even when we are unaware of, or oppose, the embodiment of God's vision in our lives and the world. Spiritually and ethically, the call forward is toward "growing in wisdom and stature," (Luke 2:52) whether it involves the twelve-year-old Jesus questioning the religious leaders in the Jerusalem Temple, a British mathematician-philosopher imagining a relational and evolving god, a French paleontologist-priest discovering divine fire in fossils, or you and me. Process theologian Bernard Loomer spoke of the human adventure in terms of size or stature:

> By size I mean the stature of a person's soul, the range and depth of his love, his capacity for relationships. I mean the volume of life you can take into your being and still maintain your integrity and individuality, the intensity and variety of outlook you can entertain in the unity of your being without feeling defensive or insecure. I mean the strength of your spirit to encourage

---

3   Whitehead, *The Adventures of Ideas*, 265.

others to become freer in the development of their diversity and uniqueness.[4]

Whether we are theologians, philosophers, business leaders, parents, or politicians, we are challenged to become cosmopolitan or large-souled persons. We are called to be people of size and stature, who embrace otherness and find a home for diverse people and opinions. The human adventure, and our own personal adventures, involve moving from isolated individualism and authoritarianism, and parochialism and exceptionalism, reflected in small ideas and backward-looking religion, to incarnate great visions of world loyalty and intellectual and spiritual adventure.

Alfred North Whitehead (1861-1947) titled one of his books *Adventures of Ideas,* and that same spirit of adventure is reflected in the lives of Whitehead and his younger contemporary, Pierre Teilhard de Chardin (1881-1955). Both pushed the boundaries of spirituality, philosophy, and science, and challenged entrenched backward-looking orthodoxies. Teilhard and Whitehead were inspired by the high hope of adventure, which led them to critique religious visions and doctrines mired in the past. Whitehead's creativity led to him becoming one of the most respected philosophers of his time. Teilhard's innovative theology led to censorship and banishment, and the modern equivalent of the Inquisition. Only after his death was Teilhard's theological and spiritual genius made known to the broader public. Together Whitehead and Teilhard are pioneers guiding us in our quest for the God of Tomorrow.

In Plato's dialogue *Phaedrus,* the philosopher Socrates comes upon young Phaedrus walking in the thoroughfares of Athens and enquires, "Where have you come from and where are you going?" Initially thinking Socrates' question is purely informational, Phaedrus recounts his activities that day. Soon, however, Socrates' walking companion realizes that the question points toward

4   Bernard Loomer, "S-I-Z-E is the Measure," in Harry James Cargas and Bernard Lee, (*Religious Experience and Process Theology.* Mahwah, NJ: Paulist Press. 1976), 70.

the origins and destiny of humankind, and the aim of human existence. He realizes that there is a Creative Wisdom moving through our lives, luring us toward realizing our destiny as children of the divine.

In the spirit of Loomer and Plato, I will give a brief account of the lives of two spiritual adventurers, both of whom were lured forward by Creative Wisdom to imagine and describe a living universe, energized by the immanent Spirit of God, and aiming toward fulfillment for person and planet alike. In a world in which many religious people try to shrink God to the size of their prejudices and comfort zones, Whitehead and Teilhard sought a divinity large enough to embrace our wildest imaginings and loving enough to welcome humankind and nature in all its wondrous diversity.

WHITEHEAD'S METAPHYSICAL JOURNEY

Generality of thought and the experience of wonder, the joining of the intimate with the Infinite with a sense of mystery and adventure, is at the heart of the philosophical journey, according to Alfred North Whitehead. In a philosophical adventure extending over six decades, Alfred North Whitehead incarnated the intellectual stature we perennially identify with the quest for wisdom found among philosophers and mystics. He was a man of two countries, both of which inspired his unique gifts. According to his collaborator in the classic *Principia Mathematica,* Bertrand Russell, "In England, Whitehead was regarded only as a mathematician and it was left to America to discover him as a philosopher."[5] An inspiration to those of us in the third act of life, Whitehead's sixties and seventies were an adventure in generativity, spaciousness of thought, and creative insight. Age is an invitation to growth in spirituality, intellect, and citizenship, in which we experience peace, as Whitehead counsels, when we evolve from self-interest to world loyalty and claim the identity of "good ancestors," com-

---

5   Victor Lowe, *Whitehead: The Man and His Work (Volume I, 1861-1910)* (Baltimore: Johns Hopkins University Press, 1985), 1.

mitted to having a positive impact on future generations, while still living on earth.

Born in Ramsgate, England, in 1861, the son of an Anglican minister and school master of the Chatham House Academy, established by Whitehead's grandfather, Whitehead had from an early age a proclivity for mathematics and the sciences. In his youth, he studied mathematics at Trinity College, Cambridge, and then taught at his alma mater Trinity College from 1884-1910. At Cambridge, he championed the admission of women to the university, at the time a losing cause. During that time, he became a celebrated mathematician as a result of his collaboration with his former student Bertrand Russell, to produce the three-volume text on the foundations of mathematics and symbolic logic, *Principia Mathematica*, published between 1910 and 1913. Whitehead concluded his British academic career as an administrator at the University of London.

At Cambridge, Whitehead's spirit and intellect expanded as a result of relationships he cultivated in his participation in the school's elite conversation society, "The Apostles." In the Society's dialogues, Whitehead responded to the question, "Shall we transcend our limitations?" with a mystical aspiration, "I want to see God." While Whitehead did not reveal his mystical experiences, Whitehead's vision of God's ever-present companionship and inspiration is the ground for affirming that there is a mystic in each and every one of us.

On more than one occasion, Whitehead affirmed that philosophy begins with wonder. As a child, Whitehead was a "quick learner," who had "a great deal of free time. Much of it was spent outdoors...He had more time than a schoolboy would have had for solitary wondering about everything he saw." Later in life, Whitehead asserted that "he was no good unless he had a couple hours each day in which he could go off by himself and think."[6] Reflection is the inspiration to creativity and service to the larger

---

6   Victor Lowe, *Whitehead: The Man and His Work* (Volume I), 32-33.

community, in Whitehead's case, through teaching and writing which has inspired creative theological visions.

Whitehead married Evelyn Wade in 1890. It is clear that this intelligent and strong-willed woman, with whom he was married nearly fifty-seven years, inspired, challenged, and deepened Whitehead's professional and philosophical life. Whitehead often acknowledged, as I do in my marriage, the significance of his marriage in shaping the contours of his intellectual life.

For a period of eight years at Cambridge, Whitehead took a great interest in theology. He even thought of converting to Roman Catholicism. Conversation companion Lucien Price notes that:

> This was all extracurricular, but so thorough that he amassed a sizable theological library. He dismissed the subject and sold the books. A Cambridge bookseller was willing to give quite a handsome figure for the collection. It then appeared that the pay must be taken in books at his shop. So he went on an orgy of book-buying until he had overdrawn his account.[7]

In his fifties, there were signs that Whitehead was reclaiming his prior interest in philosophy and religion. In 1911, Whitehead began a twelve-year stint holding professorial and administrative posts at the University of London, where he began to take serious interest in philosophy. In the wake of World War I, the death of his son Eric, as well as the loss of a generation of young men, many of whom were his students and younger colleagues, may have inspired the mathematician to seek the consolations of metaphysics and religion, the quest for something eternal in our perpetually perishing world. The tragedies of an unnecessary war, later ironically described as "the war to end all wars," brought forth a renewed interest in philosophy and theology and inspired Whitehead's vision of an intimate and relational God, "the fellow

---

7   Lucien Price, *Dialogues with Alfred North Whitehead* (Boston: Little, Brown and Company, 1954), 9.

sufferer who understands."[8] The presence of God in the world, both as the source of possibility and preservation of value, enabled Whitehead to imagine a world in which nothing is ever lost and the ambiguities of life find healing in the experience of "tragic beauty." In God's experience, our lives perish and yet live ever-more.[9]

Whitehead's mature world view and approach to truth was shaped by the collapse in the early twentieth century of Newtonian physics, which had been presumed to be the final word in describing the universe. As Whitehead notes:

> I have been fooled once and I'll be damned if I'll be fooled again! Einstein is supposed to have made an epochal discovery [demolishing Newtonian certainty]. I am respectful and interested but also skeptical. There is no more reason to expect that Einstein's relativity is anything final, than Newton's *Principia.* The danger is dogmatic thought; it plays the devil with religion; and science is not immune from it.[10]

Whitehead's experience of intellectual disillusionment inspired him to focus on adventure and novelty as essential to the practices of religion, philosophy, and science, and the flourishing of civilization. World views and religious beliefs need to be constantly open to transformation as we encounter new experiences and scientific data. Commitment to the "adventure of ideas" enlivens our intellectual and spiritual quests and invites us to explore new images of God and the world. There can never be dogmatic finality in our religious and scientific adventures. Always leave the windows of your mind open for new inspirations from God's Spirit. Always update your image of God just as you would update your computer or curriculum vitae to reflect new achievements.

---

8   Alfred North Whitehead, *Process and Reality: Corrected Edition.* (New York: Free Press, 1978), 351.

9   Ibid., 351.

10 Lucien Price, Dialogues with Alfred North Whitehead, 345-346.

The spirit of adventure applies to religion as well as science. New ideas expand our religious consciousness and the power of spirituality to transform our lives. When religion sees truth and doctrine as static and unchanging, it stifles the human spirit and becomes irrelevant to the challenges of our time.

In 1924, at age sixty-three, Whitehead was invited to join the faculty of Harvard University, where he taught in the philosophy department until 1937. As a professor at Harvard, Whitehead was set free to speculate on metaphysics, intellectual history, and religious experience, grounded in his emerging holistic vision of a philosophy of organism. He encouraged the same adventures of ideas among his students. Victor Lowe, one of Whitehead's Harvard students, and later Whitehead's biographer, notes that "everyone who knew Whitehead at Harvard immediately recalls his insistence that each student pursues those investigations which appealed to his trained instincts, not those which a professor knew to be efficiently manageable topics for theses."[11] Whitehead was well-known for placing student creativity over rigorous grading. Whitehead routinely gave higher marks to his students than his Harvard colleagues. As a university and seminary professor for over four decades, I wonder if Whitehead, the "easy" grader, intentionally sought to give his students a creative space to achieve excellence and the grace to take intellectual chances, often yielding innovative work.

Whitehead's creative and liberating spirit inspired students who would become the apostles of process theology and philosophy. The philosopher died in 1947, leaving a legacy that has transformed the spirit of theological reflection and spiritual formation, inspiring us to embody God's vision, "on earth as it is in heaven." Companioning with the adventurous God, who joins the cosmic with the personal, we incarnate divine adventure in our lives. "The vitality of thought is an adventure. That is what I have been saying

---

11 Victor Lowe, *Alfred North Whitehead: The Man and His Work (Volume I, 1861-191)*, 58.

all my life, and I have said little else. Ideas won't keep. Something must be done about them…the meaning of life is adventure."[12]

TEILHARD'S EVOLUTIONARY SPIRITUALITY

Twenty years Whitehead's junior, Pierre Teilhard de Chardin's life has been described as a "passionate intellectual and spiritual adventure…a life full of expeditions, travel, and exploration, of relentless questioning and searching for new answers, a life full of extraordinary action accompanied by deep reflection and sustained by a fervent faith."[13] A type of theological Indiana Jones!

Teilhard was born on May 1,1881 in Auvergne, Central Southern France. His father was an upper-class landowner, a country gentleman, captivated by history and nature. His mother conveyed to him her love of the Sacred Heart of Jesus and the saints and mystics of Christian history. From his childhood, Teilhard was on a spiritual-naturalistic quest to discern holiness within the world of geological formations and prehistoric species. He bathed his senses in nature and had a special affinity for rocks. It was in his native Auvergne that he first experienced "the crimson glow of matter," what he was later to describe as the "Divine radiating from the depths of blazing matter."[14]

As a child, Teilhard wrestled with the reality of mortality and the impermanence of things and sought to discover something stable in a world of perpetual change. Looking back on his childhood mysticism, Teilhard recalls that following a haircut, he placed his recently cut curls near the fire, and they were burned in less than a second. "A terrible grief assailed me; I had learned that I was perishable."[15] Like Whitehead, Teilhard sought realities that were solid, unchanging, and immortal in a world of flux.

---

12 Lucien Price, *Dialogues of Alfred North Whitehead*, 254.
13 Ursula King, *Spirit of Fire: The Life and Vision of Teilhard de Chardin* (Maryknoll, NY: Orbis Books, 2015), ix.
14 Ibid., 7.
15 Ibid., 7,

The quest for something stable in a world of perpetual change led Teilhard, as a child, to love stones and later become a geologist. At eighteen, Teilhard's quest for eternity in a changing world led him to join the Society of Jesus, the Jesuits, where one of his spiritual mentors counseled him to join the service of God through commitment to scientific studies. Thus began the spiritual adventure of bridging the gulf between faith and science and spirituality and evolution. Teilhard recognized, with the Greek pre-Socratic philosopher Heraclitus and his older contemporary Whitehead, that all things flow and that we can never step in the same waters twice; he also discovered that the flow of life was animated by the ever-present and ever-loving God, whose goal was to reconcile all things in Christ and whose energy of love propelled us toward the future. Perhaps, no one in Christian theology joined faith and evolution with the depth and passion that characterized Teilhard's work.

In 1905, Teilhard's intellectual adventures took him to Egypt, where he joined teaching and paleontology. Teilhard was thrilled when a shark fossil he found was named *Teilhardi* by the Geographical Society of France. During his sojourn in Egypt, Teilhard discovered the North African Desert Mothers and Fathers, which piqued his interest in monasticism and mysticism.

World War I was as pivotal for the theological and spiritual formation of Teilhard as it had been for the elder Whitehead. Like many of his generation, including Whitehead's son Eric, Teilhard was swept up by the winds of war. Despite his vocation as a priest, he chose to be a stretcher-bearer during World War I. Although orderlies were looked down upon by combatants, the soldier-priest Teilhard felt a solidarity with the soldiers on the front and conducted religious services and rites whenever possible. According to one biographer, "the turmoil of war clarified his inner vision. It made him realize in a new way that matter was charged with life and spirit."[16] In describing the mysticism of the earth, Teilhard asserted that "the mystic was looking for the devouring fire which

---

16 Ibid., 55.

he could identify with the Divine that summons him from all sides; science points it out to him. *See, the universe is ablaze.*"[17]

Amid the trauma and devastation of war, Teilhard discovered that God's Spirit moves quietly forward, aiming toward wholeness and complexity, with starts and stops, as it has for billions of years on earth and throughout the universe. Human hatred and violence, and human ignorance and incivility, cannot still the mystic's vision. Reflecting on his experiences of war, Teilhard arrived at a concept of beauty amid carnage similar to Whitehead's vision of tragic beauty, articulated in the final pages of the philosopher's *Adventures of Ideas.* Believing his service gave him greater stature and insight as a man and a priest, Teilhard asserted that "life is beautiful, in the grimmest circumstances – when you can see God, ever-present, in them."[18]

Following the war, Teilhard immersed himself once more in science. He believed that God is discovered both in the Catholic mass and also in the laboratory and fossil field. Just as Brother Lawrence found God's eucharistic presence in the kitchen, Teilhard discovered divinity in the study of rocks and human remains. He found study and research to be forms of prayer and windows into divine revelation and human destiny.

In 1923, Teilhard's scientific studies took him to China, where he continued his quest to experience communion with God in all things, material and spiritual, in his vocation as a researcher-priest. Just as God is found in the transformed elements of bread and cup, God is also incarnate in stone, stream, cloud, and human flesh and bone. All life is transfigured, reflecting the glory of God illuminating all things, when seen through the eyes of faith. In 1929, Teilhard participated in the discovery of the Peking Man, the fossils of which date as early as 700,000 BCE. In joining paleontology and priesthood, Teilhard experienced the Incarnation as a radical immersion in the world of matter and flesh, and not an escape from history and embodiment. With John's Gospel, Teil-

---

17 Ibid., 62,
18 Ibid., 52 Excerpt from a letter, written May 28, 1915.

hard recognized that "the Word became flesh and lived among us, and we have seen his glory, the glory as of a father's only son, full of grace and truth." (John 1:14) The Incarnation in Jesus makes all life incarnational. God is found in a Bethlehem manger, the Cross on Calvary, and the human and non-human struggle for spiritual and evolutionary transcendence.

During his first years in China, Teilhard's theological and scientific work became circulated in both religious and scientific communities, leading eventually to his censure by his religious superiors, who feared that his understanding of God's presence in the evolutionary process and physical universe threatened the traditional doctrines of the church, including the uniqueness of humankind and the doctrine of original sin. If God is the creative and wise energy inspiring the long and slow process of evolution from matter to spirit, and non-human to human, then faithful Christians must discover alternatives to literal understandings of the primordial couple Adam and Eve as well as the Genesis account of creation. Faithfulness to God calls us to forward-looking creative transformation in our understanding of God, revelation, and history, rather than backward-viewing biblical and theological fundamentalism. Moreover, if the universe is a sacrament, as Teilhard contends, then the theological implication is clear: the sacraments of religious institutions are one of many pathways to God and not the only ritual necessary for salvation. Beyond the sacraments of churches, including his own Roman Catholicism, Teilhard discovered that the whole world becomes a vehicle to salvation and its own kind of church.

Teilhard continued to research and write on the interplay of geology, paleontology, evolution, and spirituality, despite being forbidden by the Roman Catholic hierarchy to publish during his lifetime. Obedient to the Roman Catholic leadership, Teilhard, like Whitehead, nevertheless recognized that static and unimaginative dogma was the greatest enemy of a vital and relevant faith.

Until his death on Easter Sunday 1955, his work was known only through private circulations among his theological and scientific friends and colleagues. Still, Teilhard persisted in joining spirituality and science, and affirming the Divine fire and creative wisdom animating the evolutionary process. Regularly critiqued by the conservative Roman Catholic leadership, Teilhard asserted in a note: "but now I can't get away from the evidence that the moment has come when the Christian impulse should be to 'save Christ' from the hands of the clerics so that the world may be saved."[19] Despite being banned by church authorities, Teilhard's work eventually became known in the scientific community. In 1947, he was promoted by the French Foreign Affairs Ministry to be an officer in the Legion of Honor, "for outstanding services to the intellectual and scientific influence of France."[20]

Although the mystic-scientist was disappointed at the continuing refusal of church authorities to allow the publication of his scientific and theological studies and his "exile" to the United States, Teilhard remained strongly committed to his vision of a cosmic Christ. Teilhard averred, "it is utterly impossible for me not to see (and to say) what I see. And I am sure that God cannot be smaller than our biggest and wildest conceptions! Of course, I cannot print. But printing is not essential."[21] Trusting God's presence within all things and his own role in the evolution of Christianity, Teilhard could in the final years of his life affirm with all humility, "I can tell you that I now live permanently in the presence of God."[22]

Sent to be "on retreat" in the United States, Teilhard experienced the freedom of the new world, despite the constraints placed upon him by the Roman Catholic Church. He continued his research, traveling to South Africa and studying the emerging technologies, including computer science, of North America. Teilhard recognized with increasing clarity that classical Christianity lacked the theological and spiritual stature to respond to the

19 Ibid., 152.
20 Ibid., 20.
21 Ibid., 204.
22 Ibid., 217.

intellectual and spiritual needs of the contemporary world. Traditional theology is too narrow in bandwidth to contain the intellectual adventures of humanity. Christ is moving beyond the church to transform human life and the universe, and the interplay of science and religion reflects God's vision of the future.

Teilhard suffered a massive heart attack on Easter Sunday, April 10, 1955. The one who sought to resurrect Christian theology died on the day of resurrection. With his death, his works became available to the public. A lively spiritual vision, energized by God's eucharistic presence in the world of matter and the multi-billion-year evolutionary journey, inspired seekers to embrace a life-affirming, holistic spirituality, open to God's truth wherever it is found. Teilhard's universalist, trans-Christian spiritual vision reflects the wisdom of John's Gospel: "The true light, which enlightens everyone, was coming into the world" (John 1:9) bringing light to seekers everywhere, whether in the fossil field, laboratory, medical theater, or sanctuary. As one of his biographers avers, Teilhard was "truly a modern mystic who combined science and mysticism in teaching a mysticism of action and transformation by teaching 'communion with God through the world.'"[23] Teilhard reminds us that we can love God in the beauty of nature and our physical bodies, intellectual and scientific pursuits, and political involvement to save the planet and ensure justice and wellbeing for all its peoples.

The work of Whitehead and Teilhard alert us to the reality that now more than ever Christ's vision needs to be "saved" from churches for whom science and truth-seeking is an enemy and whose leaders have become apostles of power and prevarication, abandoning the way of Jesus to achieve narrow political and cultural objectives.

---

23 Ibid., 242.

Spiritual Practices: Becoming Fire

Once upon a time in a North African monastery, Abba Lot came to Abba Joseph and said: "Father, according as I am able, I keep my little rule, and my little fast, my prayer, meditation and contemplative silence; and, according as I am able, I strive to cleanse my heart of thoughts: now what more should I do?" The elder rose up in reply and stretched out his hands to heaven, and his fingers became like ten lamps of fire. He said: "Why not become fire?"

Whitehead and Teilhard are both fiery spiritual guides and wisdom givers. Teilhard was inspired by the inner fire, residing in all things and inspiring the cosmos toward Spiritual Wholeness. Whitehead spoke of the Divine Eros, luring us forward on an adventure of ideas, birthed in the intellect and then inspiring cultural and personal transformation. Teilhard and Whitehead believed that the love of wisdom begins in wonder and with wonder comes amazement and passion.

In the spirit of their integrative thought and spirituality – what I describe as "theospirituality" - each chapter concludes with spiritual practices to enliven and enlighten your theological reflections and to make the visions of Teilhard and Whitehead come alive in your own adventures of the spirit.

I believe that theological adventure is grounded in the interplay of *vision* (our world view and understanding of God's presence in the world and our lives), *promise* (the assurance that we can experience the Holy in relationship to God and the world), and *practice* (spiritual activities that open a portal to the divine presence in our lives and the world and inspire life-transforming action.) Both Whitehead and Teilhard believe that God can be experienced and that there is a hidden mystic in each of us.

Opening to the Energy of the Universe. In this spiritual practice, I invite you to reflect on and experience the energy that gave birth to the universe and still flows through us, energizing, enlivening, and enlightening. In this spiritual journey integrating metaphysics, mysticism, and mission, begin with a time of silence, breathing deeply the energies of the universe. Experience your unity with the Breath of Life with each breath. Feel the Cosmic Breath, that moved over the waters and helped light the flame of the Big Bang. Feel the whole energy of the universe flowing through you as you inhale. Then as you exhale, let the energy of the universe, described by Teilhard as the energy of love and Whitehead as the Eros of the universe, flow out from you to give energy and enlightenment to the world around you. Let the God of Tomorrow be your companion and guide.

Throughout your day, breathe deeply this Loving Energy, feeling a connection with the world far and near. Open your eyes – the eyes of the spirit – during the day to experience the inner energy of those around you, feel the flow of this holy energy within you and the world around you in the wondrous and graceful interdependence of life.

Intellectual Discord and Creative Transformation. Both Whitehead and Teilhard grew spiritually and intellectually as a result of their willingness to challenge religious and scientific dogmas and open to new ideas about God, the world, human experience, and the relationship of religion and science. Perhaps, your life has involved the deconstructing former "unquestioned" beliefs in the quest for life-giving and constructive understandings of God, suffering, and your relationship with God.

In this spiritual-intellectual exercise, begin with a time of silent reflection, opening to God's iconoclastic and inspirational presence in the world. Looking prayerfully at your life, consider the questions:

- What were your beliefs about God and the world when you were a child?

- What beliefs, if any, were "enforced" by religious authorities as essential to orthodoxy and salvation?

- When did you first experience dissonance with "established" belief systems in religion, science, culture, etc.? How did you feel at the time? How did you resolve these intellectual and ethical discords? (These discords could involve the dissonance between institutional, religious, and cultural norms or dogmas regarding the relationship of faith and science, the nature of God, other religious traditions, race, gender, or sexual identity.)

• How have you experienced the emergence of new constructive understandings of God, human existence, the world, and other issues?

• Do you have any further "growing edges" intellectually and spiritually?

Conclude your time of intellectual-spiritual reflection with a prayer, remembering that prayers don't need words but that our deepest prayers may involve a sense of openness to growth and transformation in relationship to our well-being, the well-being of those around us, and alignment with the Holy. Ask for guidance in terms of future growth, and openness to God's presence in new and possibly dissonant ideas.

2

WHITEHEAD'S METAPHYSICS OF LOVE

The teleology of the universe is directed to the production of Beauty. Thus any system of things which is in any wide sense beautiful is to that extent justified in its existence.... [God] does not create the world, he saves it: or more accurately he is the poet of the world leading it by his vision of truth, beauty, and goodness.[1]

Philosophy begins with wonder. So does theology. A child asks their grandparent why there is something rather than nothing and ponders what existed before God came to be. Later they gaze at the universe, overwhelmed by the contrast between the grandeur of the heavens and the finitude of humankind. Radical amazement, as Rabbi Abraham Heschel avers, is the origin, inspiration, and aspiration of the spiritual adventure. The universe is always more than we can imagine in size, complexity, and variety. Though we seek to tame the universe and the Creative Wisdom that gives it life through doctrines and institutions, the universe and its Creator always breaks free beyond our control and concepts. Neither science nor religion stand still, nor does God the Creative Wisdom of the Universe. God is always more than we can imagine. God's creativity and love amaze and astound us. We cannot comprehend the depth and breadth of divinity. God's iconoclastic spirit – and God is the ultimate iconoclast as well as preserver of the best of our traditions - always shatters our doctrinal certainties and breaks through our theological boundaries.

---

1 Whitehead, *Adventures of Ideas,* 265 and *Process and Reality,* 346.

In those moments when we simply open ourselves to the wonder of all being and becoming, we find holiness and inspiration, awe, and sometimes terror, in all things. We see the "tree with lights," gleaming and enlightening with Annie Dillard, admire intelligence in a "considerable speck," a mite running across a sheet of paper, with Robert Frost, and find ourselves awestruck as we lay on the ground transfixed by a grasshopper chewing a blade of grass on a summer day with Mary Oliver. We discover that we are "awesomely and wonderfully made," with the author of Psalm 139, as we ponder the human spirit, the untrammeled imagination, and the cells of our bodies. Caught between the miraculous world of macro and the micro, we stammer with the Psalmist:

> O Lord, our Sovereign,
>   how majestic is your name in all the earth!
> You have set your glory above the heavens.
>
> Out of the mouths of babes and infants
> you have founded a bulwark because of your foes,
>   to silence the enemy and the avenger.
>
> When I look at your heavens, the work of your fingers,
>   the moon and the stars that you have established;
> what are humans that you are mindful of them,
>   mortals that you care for them? (Psalm 8:1-4)

We burst forth with a song of my childhood days in a small-town Baptist church, "How Great Thou Art," and then look in the mirror and discover the wonder of our own being and the vast responsibilities of life and death with which the interplay of divine wisdom and the evolutionary process, along with our parents' choices, have endowed us. Star stuff or God stuff or Earth stuff, or the combination of all three in the wondrous adventures of Spirit:

> Yet you have made them a little lower than God
>   and crowned them with glory and honor.
> You have given them dominion over the works of your
> hands. (Psalm 8:5-6)

Then, lest we think we are the crown of creation, somehow disconnected in complexity, creativity, value, and wonder from the non-human world, the Psalmist returns to the Ground of Wonder. We are children of earth as well as heaven. Our destiny is to build the earth so that it reflects God's creative vision.

> O Lord, our Sovereign,
>   how majestic is your name in all the earth! (Psalm 8:9)

Despite our limitations and tendency to privilege abstract doctrines over concrete spiritual experience, and self-interest over world loyalty, philosophy and theology matter. The most insightful theologians and philosophers live between silence and speech and infinity and finitude and in that tension follow the counsel of poet Mary Oliver, "Pay Attention. Be astonished. Tell about it."[2]

Theology and philosophy emerge from mystical experiences. The great religions began with mysticism not doctrine – Mary of Nazareth's encounter with the angel Gabriel, the descent of the dove at Jesus' baptism, Moses and the burning bush, Peter's dream of the smorgasbord of unclean food, Mary of Magdala hearing her name called in the Garden. These experiences of immanence and transcendence heal, unite, and energize. We describe the Holy, and yet confess that our descriptions are finite. We revel in wonder and must share our wonder in words and images, knowing that none of them can contain or describe the Living God or the person sleeping next to us, in my case, my companion of forty-five years Kate. Mary Oliver spends an afternoon pondering the amazing complexity of a grasshopper, and then asks herself and her readers to ponder the amazing complexity of their own

---

2   Mary Oliver, "Sometimes," *Devotions: The Selected Poems of Mary Oliver* (New York: Penguin Books, 2017), 104-106.

unique, wild, and unrepeatable lives.[3] Such contemplation of the
wildness and wonder of life, the amazing complexity of our finite
lives, enlivens our spirits and serves as an antidote to static and
authoritarian religion.

My theological and spiritual journey has been inspired by a
phrase attributed to a variety of theologians and philosophers from
the Pre-Socratics to Bonaventure and Nicholas of Cusa: "God is
a circle (or infinite sphere) whose center is everywhere and whose
circumference is nowhere." In many ways, if we add the spirit
of relatedness and dynamism to this affirmation, we capture the
heart of Whitehead's and Teilhard's vision of the universe.

The God of Jesus, Whitehead, Teilhard, and the mystics is
present everywhere. Every moment reflects divine creativity and
wisdom. Every moment is energized by the divine energy of love.
Although we may turn away from our relationship to Creative
Wisdom, God still centers us. Wherever we are, God is present.
The moral and spiritual arcs of the universe flow through us and
everything else in the wondrous adventure of divine incarnation.

The circumference of God's loving creativity is nowhere. All
things are filled and embraced by divine love. As the vision of
panentheism affirms:

> God in all things.
> All things in God.

The fountain of divine love flows through all things, as the
Franciscan philosopher Bonaventure affirms, and all things flow
back into God. The God, whose circumference is nowhere and
agency and creativity are everywhere, inspires a democracy of
revelation in which all things are words of God and God's light
enlightens everyone. Still reaching toward beauty and wholeness,
incomplete and restless, the world leans in the direction of greater
beauty and Christ consciousness. God is in this place, right where
we are, as we, like the Hebraic patriarch Jacob, wake up amazed
from a dream in which heaven and earth are joined and experience

3   Mary Oliver, "The Summer Day." *Devotions,* 316.

the holiness of all creation and the ever-flowing stream of divine creativity. There is a ladder of angels everywhere, and the world around us bursts forth with revelatory possibilities.

Whitehead and Teilhard were philosopher-theologians and spiritual guides who were inspired by the ever-evolving and ever-encompassing divine circle. Wonder, beauty, and love, and the vision of a personal universe center their world view. Although they had slightly different foci – physics and biology, respectively - and visions of the goal of history, Whitehead and Teilhard share a vision of a living, evolving, energetic universe. A universe that is going somewhere, even if the nature and goal of the journey is open-ended, not fully known by us or God. Inspired by wonder, they sought to bring that spirit of wonder to metaphysics and religion and to energize a religion stifled by its fixation on yesterday's dogmas and a value-free science.

In Chapters Two and Three, I will describe the contours of Whitehead's and Teilhard's metaphysical visions. My vocation in both chapters, which are the theological heart of this book, is to provide a vision that will undergird and inspire both a mystic vision and an earth transforming mission. My approach will be more cosmological and spiritual, more evocative and poetic, than analytic. Analysis is important, but energizing the journey of philosophical reasoning is the experience of wonder, beauty, meaning, and value, flowing through our lives and the universe, and undergirding our science and theology. Metaphysical and theological reflection, as Whitehead notes, is as much akin to poetry as analysis. We discern the nature of the universe as much in dreams, visions, and emotions as we do in doctrines and formulae. Mystics and poets often guide theologians and scientists in the quest for truth and beauty.

WHITEHEAD'S EMPATHETIC UNIVERSE

As I child, I took great comfort in Maltbie Babcock's hymn, "This is My Father's World." While the most progressive among us appropriately update the hymn's language to go beyond binary and dualistic categories of gender, and substitute "parent" or "creator," Babcock's hymn describes the energetic, evolving, and empathetic universe portrayed by Alfred North Whitehead and Teilhard de Chardin.

> This is my Father's world,
> And to my listening ears
> All nature sings, and round me rings
> The music of the spheres.
>
> This is my Father's world:
> I rest me in the thought
> Of rocks and trees, of skies and seas;
> His hand the wonders wrought.
>
> This is my Father's world,
> The birds their carols raise,
> The morning light, the lily white,
> Declare their maker's praise.
>
> This is my Father's world,
> He shines in all that's fair;
> In the rustling grass I hear Him pass;
> He speaks to me everywhere.

Though steeped in mathematics and physics, Alfred North Whitehead was a prophet of cosmic re-enchantment. The universe is alive. Evolution is an adventure in aesthetic achievement and novelty. Creation is composed of drops of experience, arising from and shaping their environment. In Whitehead's pan-experiential world, feeling is at the heart of reality. In the spirit of Celtic sages, Whitehead recognizes with the Celtic spiritual guides that there are "thin places" everywhere, in which God and the world meet and sing together hymns of creative transformation. The heavens declare the glory of God and so do the birds of the air, the lilies of the field, the grasshopper munching grass, and the cells of our bodies. The Hubble and Webb telescopes reveal a universe that bursts forth with beauty and so do magnified photos of T-cells fighting disease within our bodies. We can embrace technological advances and, at the same time, cultivate experiences of beauty, wonder, and appreciation of a living, creative, and purposive universe. "In rustling grass, we hear God pass. God speaks to us everywhere."

God is not aloof and absent from the universe. God is the energy of love, giving life and motion to the universe and seeking beauty in every encounter. The world is charged with God's grandeur and lives by the incarnation of God in each moment and in the long haul of the evolutionary process. The Word is made flesh in Bethlehem's stable and also in the birth of a galaxy.

In Whitehead's world, mystics can be scientists and scientists can be mystics. Although Whitehead's opus *Process and Reality* is chock full with incomprehensible language, beneath Whitehead's challenging communication – the result, in part, of his recognition that the world view he was presenting was novel and innovative – poetry abounds and the intellectual artistry reflects the inspiration of the Poet of the Universe, who elicits beauty from the tragedies of life and treasures each occasion in God's evolving and expanding remembrance of the universe.

Whitehead observes that the evolving universe is not result of mechanistic interactions of unfeeling and purposeless matter in motion and isolated and independent atoms, as materialists and Newtonian-influenced deists believe, but reflects an inner Eros and emotional energy that births forth the dynamic interdependence of life, the universality of experience, and the evolution of galaxies, planets, and the human adventure.

In the following sections, I will describe the contours of Whitehead's empathetic, evolving, and erotic universe in everyday language and the imagery of artists, mystics, and poets as well as theologians and scientists. I will leave the fine points of Whitehead's thought – how many actual entities can dance on the head of a pin or the origin or the metaphysical location of eternal objects in God's experience and the world – to more scholastic oriented writers. Scholasticism and textual analysis are necessary to clarify the perspectives of philosophers and theologians, but our scholastic ruminations emerge from and must return to passion and imagination, and wonder at this wild, wonderful, and dynamic universe.

In Whitehead's spirit, I want to paint a picture of an alternative metaphysical vision to the cosmic and theological individualism, mechanism, lifelessness, and supernaturalism privileged by many in the scientific, economic, and religious world. A living empathetic universe inspires the vision of a living, embodied, immanent, creative, evolving, and relational God, whose creativity brings forth naturalistic miracles each moment of the day. We can experience divine creativity and evolution in the world around us and in our own creativity and spiritual growth.

We can, as Teilhard also affirms, claim our vocation as God's partners in evolving the world as a counterforce to the forces of entropy and destruction in the body politic and the larger universe.

Empathy, evolution, and pan-experientialism. The universe is alive and evolving! Whitehead's empathetic universe is made up of lively, complex, and interdependent drops of experience, also described by the philosopher as actual entities, actual occasions, or occasions of experience. The stable world of experience arises from lively and creative energy events that "prehend," feel, or embrace the universe from which they arise and within their brief moment of creativity shape their experience of the universe guided implicitly by an inner passion. Then, as completed entities, become factors in the ongoing history of their immediate environment and the universe. Regardless how complex these occasions of experience may be, the same truth applies to all creation: "the primitive element is sympathy, that is, feeling the feelings in another and feeling conformally with another"[4]

4   Whitehead, *Process and Reality,* 162.

The stable world of perception and manipulation, composed of a myriad of these occasions of experience bonded together by common aims and possibilities, necessary for the stable foundations of daily life and future planning, is also, despite appearances, alive, energetic, passionate, and constantly arising and perishing. What appears to be stability emerges from the interplay of these momentary occasions of experience, or actual entities, with their environment, grounded in a common and enduring (sometimes only for a few moments) vision or character that unites them with a myriad of other energy events to form the interdependent and socially organized societies of atoms, cells, rocks, trees, bodily organs, and animal bodies that provide order, permanence, predictability, and continuity to our daily lives.

Each moment and the universe as a whole are held together by relational feelings and experiential responses. What we feel moment by moment is mirrored in the primitive experiences of the occasions that compose our bodily cells, flora and fauna, and the bodies of our non-human companions, be they mammals, fish, birds, or insects. What we call matter is profoundly alive and energetic from the simplest to the most complex physical entities. Deep down, all occasions of experience are energized by an inner eros, a divine passionate possibility congruent with their environment and immediate context, aiming at complexity and intensity in this moment and as a gift to the future. While occasions of experience vary in complexity, intensity, and environmental sensitivity, each moment of experience aims, as Whitehead notes, to be part of larger process grounded in the individual and cosmic goal "to live, to live well, to live better" in its brief moment of existence and its enduring impact on its immediate successors, environment, and God.[5]

Whitehead's vision joins the fruits of biology, physics, and cosmology with the enchanted world of mystics, spiritual teachers, indigenous people, and Romantic poets. The heavens truly declare

---

5   Alfred North Whitehead, *The Function of Reason* (Boston: Beacon Press, 1969).

the glory of God. The universe pours forth speech. Pangolins and Right Whales experience and embody divine purpose. My ninety-five-pound Golden Doodle has passions and preferences, emotions and memories, that can't be reduced to stimulus-response. The societies of occasions of experience, joined by common character-istics and aims – eternal objects arising from God's "primordial," unchanging, and imaginative, nature in Whitehead's language – that comprise the flowers on our townhouse patio reach out to bees in search of pollination. Nature is alive, and out of lively movements of nature, occurring over millions of years, emerge animals, proto-humans, and the human adventure of civilization reaching toward the stars. The poetry of the Psalms reflects what Gerard Manley Hopkins describes as the "dearest freshness deep down things" of which we are a part and from which we receive life.[6] Indeed, the words of Psalm 148 summarize the emotive and passionate world vision of Whitehead and Teilhard.

> Praise the Lord from the earth,
>   you sea monsters and all deeps,
> fire and hail, snow and frost,
> stormy wind fulfilling his command!
>
> Mountains and all hills,
>   fruit trees and all cedars!
> Wild animals and all cattle,
>   creeping things and flying birds! (Psalm 148:9-10)

A world of empathy is a world of praise, and a democracy of revelation! We are not alone in a silent universe. We are alive, as spiritual and metaphysical companions of all nature, embedded in an evolving and experiencing universe, a feeling universe, in which deep down, everything that breathes praises God. (Psalm 150:6)

Interdependence and relationship. Whitehead charts a meta-physics of feeling and experience that binds together the universe

---

6   Gerard Manley Hopkins, "God's Grandeur."

in the microcosm and macrocosm. The whole universe, the philosopher asserts, conspires to create each moment of experience. The affirmation *Ubuntu,* a mantra for relational theologies such as Teilhard's, Whitehead's, and mine: "I am because of you, we are because of one another," applies to every level of the universe. In Whitehead's world, there is no "simple location," no isolated atom, no rugged individualist, or "self-made man." Each moment of life emerges from the universe and flows back into the universe, its life a gift to the ongoing processes of evolution.

Whitehead asserts that we cannot find an ultimate boundary between the universe and our bodies and mental experience. Indeed, in an experiential as well as poetic way, the world is our body and the world gives birth to each moment of experience, from which my creativity emerges. Whitehead avers that "the world beyond is so intimately entwined in our own natures that unconsciously we identify our more vivid experiences with it." Pondering the intricate interdependence of life, the philosopher speculates that "the body is part of the external world, continuous with it. In fact, it is as much part of nature as anything else there – a river, or a mountain, or a cloud. Also, if we are fussily exact, we cannot define where a body begins and the external world of nature ends."[7]

Looking at my own quotidian experience as a portal into the nature of things, I discover that as I write this morning, experientially speaking, I and the computer are one. I feel the refreshing and unexpected coolness of an August morning in Potomac, Maryland. My senses are shaped not only by the computer screen and the interaction of my fingers with the keyboard, but the ambient quiet of the predawn suburbia and the glimmers of light entering through my study window. I and my arts and crafts chair are one, despite the different cellular structures and complexity that characterize our two realities. I feel the stability of the chair, its comfort, and the relaxation response that emerges immediately as

---

7   Alfred North Whitehead, *Modes of Thought* (New York: Free Press, 1966), 21.

a result of years of typing and reading supported by its stability. I hear the coffee dripping in the kitchen, eliciting another form of the relaxation response that comes from the lifelong pleasure I anticipate from imbibing a strong cup of coffee in between tapping on my laptop or reading a book. In a few minutes, I will reward myself with a daily predawn walk – I awaken around 4:30 a.m. each morning! – feasting my senses on the varied beauties of our arboreal neighborhood, enchanted by the stillness, almost silence, of the Maryland suburbs soon to be shattered by the whizzing cars and lumbering school buses as the nation's capital begins the workday.

Far from the soon to be bustling Washington DC suburbs, when I walk Cape Cod beaches on holiday, "wandering lonely as a cloud," I am all eye and all sense, as the North Africans Desert Parents described the most perceptive monks and can barely tell the difference between the sand between my toes, the crashing waves, the gentle breeze, and my own thoughts and emotions. I am the beach and the beach is me.[8] I am the quiet neighborhood and in predawn stillness I experience the unity of creation. In the interdependent universe that Whitehead envisions there is no "other." We are each unique and also connected, whether we speak of the cells of our bodies, the relationship of persons, the ebb and flow of conversation, the impact of toxins in the environment, or the activities of nations. As Whitehead describes, "each creative act is the universe incarnating itself as one."[9] The environment supplies and determines the quality of my experience. In the concreteness and limitations provided by the environment, possibility and agency emerge.

Dynamic Process. "Panta rei", "everything flows," so announced the Pre-Socratic philosopher Heraclitus of Ephesus (circa 500 BCE). Life is an ever-flowing stream giving birth to all creation. Not only the universe, but God is in constant motion. Whitehead imagines God to be the primary agent of change, the source of

---

8   William Wordsworth, "I Wandered Lonely as a Cloud."

9   Whitehead, *Process and Reality,* 245.

possibility in the emerging world and the recipient of the changing world's achievements in God's evolving and growing experience of the universe. Supplanting Aristotle's passionless and apathetic unmoved mover, Whitehead envisions God as the "most
moved mover," a phrase coined by Abraham Joshua Heschel and
employed by process philosopher Charles Hartshorne, and the
source of novelty as well as order. God is, as Bonaventure affirms,
a constantly flowing fountain of love filling the universe with life,
order, and novelty. Within the rapids of change, birth, and death,
there are realities that are infinite, eternal, and unchanging. While
abstract apart from process, God's knowledge, creativity, impact,
and existence is infinite, unchanging, and eternal. God is faithful
and loving in every season of life and pathway of evolution.

God's vision of possibility, described by Whitehead in terms
of God's primordial envisagement of eternal objects, is all-encompassing and eternal, although these eternal possibilities are meaningful only in relationship to concrete occasions of experience.
Although I am at variance with some Whiteheadian interpreta-
tions of the nature of eternal objects, I have come to believe that
the realm of eternal objects, described as the "primordial nature of
God" represents in a poetic way God's dream for the universe and
each creature, part and whole, a dream that is relativized, concret-
ized, and embodied in the flux of experience, embraced by what
Whitehead describes as God's "consequent nature." Though con-
textualized and modified in the universe of change, God's dream
of Beauty and Shalom still lives on as the Eros of the Universe.
In relationship to the ever-flowing stream of process, the eternity
of divine wisdom and possibility becomes fully alive, arising and
perishing, in the adventure of individual and cosmic evolution.

The process is the reality and the reality is adventurous. Each
moment of experience arises, perishes, and gives birth to the
future beyond itself, whether it be a drop of experience in cellular life or the calculations of a physicist at Los Alamos. In small
and large ways, we shape the process in each moment, creating or
destroying, inspiring or stifling the future. Humankind's "adven-

tures of ideas" reflects God's dynamic and interpersonal cosmic and intimate creativity. God has "ideas" and emotions too and they constantly flow in and through God's experience, eventuating in God's transformative presence in the world of change.

While not predetermined, each moment in the flow of life has an inner telos or eschaton toward which it aims. The eschaton toward which each occasion aims is not the end of the process, but the pathway to further adventures. The world process itself arcs toward greater complexity and intensity of experience and a creative interplay of chance, order, and purpose. God is constantly evolving the world and human existence in the call and response of divine wisdom and human freedom. The universal aim toward wholeness and beauty is the source of hope in the individual moment and the long haul of history. To the surprise of many traditional theologians, God's prophetic vision may also be the source of chaos and unrest as a result of God's presentation of alternatives to the unjust status quo and theological fixations on yesterday's God.

Value Everywhere. We are always on holy ground! A world of experience is a world of value. To feel and create is to be a locus of value, worthy of ethical consideration. In contrast to the modern world view's exorcism of value from the "material" and "non-human world" and its assertion that non-humans, whether flora, fauna, or geological, have value only in relationship to human interests, Whitehead affirms that every creature has value for itself and for the world. Within every creature is an eros toward beauty and intensity of experience, reflective of God's vision. God's incarnate vision, or "initial aim," gives birth to each moment of experience, and even when creatures fail to achieve their purpose or turn, as we often do, from light to darkness, and generosity to self-interest, they are still the object of God's care. The non-human world is essential to human well-being and has value apart from our interests. To exist is to experience and to be a center of value, unique and holy.

The experience of value in the world beyond ourselves and transcending human machinations and purposes awakens us to the holiness of life and ethical consideration of the non-human world and our own human kin. According to Whitehead, the aesthetic or valuational nature of life:

> arouses an awakening to the sublime value of nature, a consciousness of holiness without which civilization is doomed to fail. When we survey nature and think however flitting and superficial has been the animal enjoyment of its wonders, and when we realize how incapable the separate cells and pulsations of each flower are of enjoying the total effect—then our sense of the value of the details for the totality dawns upon our consciousness. This is the intuition of holiness, the intuition of the sacred, which is at the foundation of all religion. In every advancing civilization this sense of sacredness has found vigorous expression.[10]

As we will see later in this text, the universality of value evokes the universality of ethical consideration at the micro and macro levels of existence.

The Universality of Creativity and Freedom. We are artists and poets of experience. To be is to create. Although the whole universe and most particularly the immediate environment and God's vision of possibility gives birth to each occasion of experience, each occasion is a center of self-creativity synthesizing the many influences into an aesthetic whole, which becomes its unique contribution to the ongoing universe. The concrete limitations of the environment are the source of possibility and inspiration and the foundation of the freedom characteristic of each moment of experience. Each moment's freedom is minimal . But over time – and in unique moments of creative decision-making – we have the freedom to transform our lives and the world around us. The

---

10 Whitehead, *Modes of Thought*, 120.

future is open for us, our institutions and communities, the planet, and God.

God has a vision of the future, but God's relational vision – God's vision for this particular time and place - is always embodied in and shaped by the moment-by-moment decisions of creatures. Although God charts the moral and spiritual arcs of the universe and human history, there is no predetermined outcome for our lives or the universe. God calls and we respond, opening God and the world to new possibilities for creative transformation and divine activity. Like the "choose your own adventure" books I read with my elementary school son in the 1980's, every choice we make leads to new possibilities and pathways of creativity for God and ourselves. God is infinitely responsive and adaptable to us and the world in which we live.

According to Whitehead, there is no final predetermined goal to the creative process and divine activity. God's vision, motivated by God's aim at truth, beauty, and goodness, is always relative to the world that is emerging at this moment and aiming toward future horizons. Many wonderful outcomes are possible as God seeks the best of all worlds in relationship to creaturely freedom, chance, and accident. God and the world innovate in the quest for beauty of experience and environment. Creativity and value are universal and reflect the inherent value of each moment of experience – and complex creature – for itself and the ongoing universe.

A Purposive Universe. God has a dream for you and the cosmos! Traditional theologies as well as dualistic philosophies assert that authentic purpose only applies to God and humankind. From the vantage point of traditional or classical theology, the rest of the universe, including our bodies and non-human animals, is mechanistic, totally controlled by instinct and stimulus response. It is just a short step from asserting that our bodies are mechanistic and purposeless to claiming that what we call our minds is merely the result of behaviorist stimulus-response or the result of firing neurons in our brains. In contrast, Whitehead affirms both universal and local purposes, emerging from God's loving imagination. Whitehead notes the irony of a scientist animated by the purpose of proving there is no purpose to the universe or themselves![11]

Purpose and intentionality, Whitehead believes, are universal and local, short and long term. The teleology of the universe aims at beauty and this quest for beauty – harmony, intensity, variety – is reflected in both the micro and macro. Every moment of experience is purposive in nature and reflects in its own process of self-creation its response to God's overarching aim at beauty and God's particular purpose for it in its brief moment of experience. God calls and we respond in every moment of experience. God's visions, embodied and shaped by the creaturely world from quarks to angels, give birth and energy to our visions and make room for our creativity. The divine initial aim, the best that particular impasse, inspires our own subjective aims, which shape our embodiment of God's vision.

God leaves room for, inspires, and delights in creaturely creativity. In the call and response of the universe, God's overarching aims for the cosmos and each individual creature and its environment are both long-term – in human life, we refer to this as "vocation," "mission," and "calling" - and immediate, relating to this particular moment.

While God may have an ideal for the universe embedded in the abstract realm of God's "primordial nature," in the flow of life, the concrete world in which we and God interact, divine and creaturely purposes are constantly changing. Accordingly, from Whitehead's perspective – and this needs to be repeated - there is no predetermined end to the cosmic process. Rather, the ideal divine vision of Shalom or Beauty, the eschaton, is incarnate in each moment and in the evolving universe with particular realizations of divine beauty being superseded by future incarnations of divine creativity and creaturely response on the galactic, solar, planetary, cultural, and personal levels of existence. In the call and

---

11 Whitehead, *The Function of Reason*, 16.

response of divine purpose and creativity, the world evolves and, tragically retreats, as a result of our decisions. Still God persists guided by God's vision of truth, beauty, and goodness. God's "purpose in the world is quality of attainment…embodied in particular ideals relevant to the actual state of the world…every act leaves the world with a deeper or fainter impress of God. He then passes into his next relation to the world with enlarged, or diminished, presentation of ideal values."[12]

A Relational, Empathetic, Creative, and Evolutionary God. And the word was made flesh! And the wisdom of God dwells right where in the messiness, complexity, and ecstasy of life! Whitehead envisions God as profoundly embedded in the universe. God exists in a symbiotic relationship with the world. In some way or other, God has always been creating and God has always had a world with which to interact. The world reflects God's nature and, more controversial to traditional theists, God reflects the world's nature. Divine-world interaction requires that God and the world be compatible and congruent in creativity and responsiveness. Although God is more than the world, God is not a stranger on the outside looking in and supernaturally intervening from time to time to rescue humankind. God's relationship to the world is similar to the relationship of spirit or mind with the body, moving within the universe, shaping and being shaped by the universe, part and whole. As Philippians 2:5-11 asserts, God saves the world by becoming part of the world and reflecting the ebb and flow divine-world relationship in God's very existence. Put more philosophically, Whitehead states that "God is not to be treated as an exception to the metaphysical principles, invoked to save their collapse. He is their chief exemplification."[13]

The world lives by the incarnation of God and God "lives" by loving intimacy with the creative advance of the world. God's love, as David Griffin and John Cobb assert, is both creative and

---

12 Whitehead, *Religion in the Making,* 152.

13 Alfred North Whitehead, *Process and Reality: Corrected Edition,* ed. David Ray Griffin, (New York: Free Press, 1978), 343.

responsive, and transcendent and immanent. In the spirit of Joan Osborne, while God is more than the world as panentheism asserts, God is also "one of us." The words "there is no other" apply to God as well as the interdependent nature of the universe. God is "with" and "within" all things, and all things are "with" and "within" God. As the word "panentheism" affirms, "God in all things, and all things in God" seamlessly and holistically.

As the primary exemplification of the Universal Creativity – and to be an exemplification does not nullify God's eternity and infinity as well as unique character as cosmic and intimate source of beauty and love – God is characterized by interdependence, artistry, growth, adventure, personality, and freedom. God has purposes and these purposes, momentary and long-term, micro and macro, are embodied in the ongoing history of the universe, political institutions, and human decisions. Although God is the primary factor in the evolutionary process, God's creativity does not predetermine or control the emerging contours of the creative process.

Accidents happen to God, too! And, God must deal with alterations to God's vision on a moment-by-moment and long-term basis. Rather than controlling everything that occurs, God inspires and guides, energizes and enlivens, the cosmic adventure and our own creaturely adventures. God rules by the power of love and inspiration not coercion and domination. God calls and the universe in its myriad occasions responds. God's call is to more, rather than less, creativity in the creaturely world and evolutionary process.

Whitehead's understanding of the God-world relationship in the microcosm of human, non-human, and quantum experience and the macrocosm of planetary and cosmic evolution can be understood in terms of his reinterpretation of the "three O's" – omnipresence, omniscience, and omnipotence – each of which reveals a different aspect of God's love for our world.

God's omnipresence reflects God's intimacy with all things. God's intimacy is both "within" and "without." God is as near as my next breath and God's energy beats with every heartbeat. "Where can I go from God's Spirit? If I ascend to heavens, you are there. If I make my bed in Sheol, you are there" (Psalm 139:8). Wherever we are – and wherever everything is in our amazing evolving, and often tragic universe – God is present. We live in a God-filled universe, from quanta and cell to the human spirit and the movements of galaxies. God is not an external observer but an intimate companion. Although each creature, including God, is a center of experience with its own integrity, freedom, and creativity, we cannot ultimately distinguish the place where we begin and God ends. This is not traditional pantheism, suggesting an absolute correspondence of God and the world, but a dynamic relationship in which each party permeates and yet cannot be reduced to its companion.

God's omniscience is God's complete and expanding awareness of the world as it emerges. "Search me and know me," the Psalmist avers. (Psalm 139:1) We are truly known and truly loved by God. God's intimate awareness of the world evolves with the world. God shapes the world and the world shapes God. This is at the heart of what the evangelicals of my childhood and the mystics throughout history describe as a "personal relationship" with God. God hears our prayers, delights in our achievements, and feels our pain. "God is the fellow sufferer who understands" and the joyful companion who celebrates and loves.

God's knowledge of the world is constantly changing and growing. This is a significant departure from traditional theism's affirmation that God knows everything in advance and that, accordingly, nothing new happens to God. Exalting changelessness over process and eternity over time, traditional theism describes God as complete in every way, and believes that any change in God is a fall from perfection. From this traditional perspective, nothing surprises God, nor can God input new experiences or exercise novel agency. Yet, a God for whom nothing new happens can never grow nor can God act in any meaningful way. Nor can such a god be the living God of prophets, mystics, and Jesus. To a

God who knows everything in advance, our prayers are of no significance nor does our pain and pleasure matter. A fully complete apathetic and unchanging God is no more living than a stone; in fact, in Whitehead's universe, a stone, or rather the components of a stone, have more vivacity than the unchanging deity. What we do makes no existential difference to the unchanging God since God already knows the outcome of each action and the totality of our lives. God has neither compassion nor passion if the world is the predetermined reflection of divine choice.

Whitehead's image of divine omniscience, identified with God's "consequent nature," does not suggest that God lacks awareness of the future. In the most comprehensive way possible, God knows future in terms of possibility, of that which emerges in the next moment or in the span of history. God knows virtually all the outcomes of a particular action or the future of our planet, but God's knowledge of the present and future is neither coercive nor actual. It is anticipatory, probable, and possible, and possibilities can be altered by both God and us. The Bible describes God changing his mind in response to the changed behaviors of the previously godless Ninevites. Jesus ponders an alternative future to the way of the cross and chooses to follow God's vision despite the painful future that lies ahead. What occurs will be known in its entirety by God when it happens and not before.

God's consequent nature, or evolving relational omniscience, unfolds as the world unfolds. Yet, unlike us, God preserves in God's experience everything that happens. Our lives perish and live evermore in God's experience. Nothing is forgotten or lost. We may forget, but God never forgets. God uses the materials of our lives, the beauty and the wreckage, to shape the future in companionship with the world.

Theologian Thomas Oord suggests that we replace the word "omnipotence" with "amipotence" to emphasize that God's power is always relational and loving.[14] From Whitehead's perspective,

---

14 Thomas Jay Oord, *The Death of Omnipotence and the Birth of Amipotence* (Nampa, ID, 2023).

God does not control the world, nor is divine causation unilateral. Divine creativity is relational, working with and within the world as it is and has been to embody God's moral and spiritual arc in its evolutionary future. Although God's power is global and persistent, God does not absolutely control any moment of experience or the process of evolution as a whole. God's presence is eschatological in so far as God aims within the evolutionary process toward the production of beauty along with intensity and complexity of experience one moment at a time and over the wide expanse of planetary and cosmic history. God's future vision is always embodied as a relational power within the world and not a compelling external force. While much theology has been motivated by the love of power, whether in terms of God's activity in the world, the authority the God's appointed churches and anointed ecclesiastical leaders, the divine right of kings, or devotion to a fallible politician, Whitehead asserts that God "rules" by the power of love. God is known by goodness not power and love not destruction. Tragically, too often religious institutions have seen God in terms of the power of Caesar, controlling, dominating, and punitive, and not the power of Jesus, loving, relational, and healing, and in times of conflict, they have jettisoned the way of Jesus for the dominance of Caesar.

The authoritarian and unilateral God is the intentional source of both good and evil and the primary inspiration and justification for authoritarian church leadership and political decision-making.

From the perspective of unilateral causation, Reformed theologian John Calvin can assert that not a leaf falls or a president is elected without God's will. As agents of the all-powerful God, we are God's instruments in the world having no agency of our own. The keys to the kingdom are ours and we have the right to excommunicate heretics, displace indigenous people, demonize political and religious opponents, storm the USA Capitol, and destroy "otherness" whether it be literature we object to or persons who fall out of our God's vision of sexual norms. The authoritarian God and his authoritarian minions rule by fear and marginalization and see otherness as a threat. We bow our knees or assent to God's appointed authorities to escape punishment or receive the perquisites of loyalty. In contrast, the relational God is out to love us, not out to get us. We bow our knees in gratitude and appreciation for the love we have received and in preparation for widening the circles of love in our world.

Although Whitehead's focus on cosmic and planetary evolution is less central to his thought than it is in Teilhard's, it is clear that the empathetic and relational God that the philosopher envisions evolves the world out of love. Evolution is the word made flesh in the flow of time and space, and like a good parent, God nurtures the world, accepting its imperfection, inspiring and working within the quest for progress, and responding to the world as it is in terms of what it can be. Infinitely resourceful, God has many images of our planetary, personal and cosmic future, all of which will bring beauty and wholeness to the world and ourselves. Yet, God's quest for wholeness is never ending. God's holy adventure in companionship with the world has no terminus point. New embodiments of order and novelty, love and creativity, lure us toward the expanding horizons of God's love.

An Evolving Universe and Its God. Whitehead describes the evolutionary process as the ongoing movement from simplicity to complexity and intensity of experience. The teleology, the aim and movement, of the universe is aimed at the production of beauty, arising from complexity, intensity, and harmony of experience. Religions evolve and so do species. Human civilization is an "adventure of ideas" reflecting the interplay of divine creativity and human response at every level of existence. The "pure conservative," whether in religion, politics, or interpersonal relationships, is going against the nature of the universe, which is to change, grow, and evolve.

Flora and fauna, and animal species evolve because of the interplay of adapting to their environment and responding to God's presence moving them and the universe forward. Evolution is not merely mechanical nor is entirely the result of the struggle for survival. Rather, the purposes we experience in our own personal evolution – "growing in wisdom and stature" – are present everywhere in the universe, albeit often in primitive forms. In the continuity of life, we can view evolution in terms of mechanical, stimulus-response causation, or view evolution as reflective of purpose and intentionality. We can view the higher levels of experience in terms of the lower, or we can envision the lower, less innovative levels of experience, in terms of aiming toward the higher levels of experience. We can understand the forces of evolution as reflecting both cooperation and competition.

There is a counterforce within the universe to entropy and mechanism. Whitehead counsels scientist and theologian alike, "Again we are told that we should look at the matter historically. [Humanity] has gradually developed from the lowliest forms of life, and must therefore be explained in terms applicable to all such forms. But why construe the later forms by analogy to the earlier forms. Why not reverse the process? It would seem to be more sensible, more truly empirical, to allow each living species to make its own contribution to the demonstration of factors inherent in living things."[15]

Deep down, God is the primary agent of evolution. The world reflects discord and the conflict between one species and another. Discord also occurs as creatures seek to be more in tune with the divine aim at beauty and intensity of experience and consciously or unconsciously challenge established behaviors and rituals. Suffering and pain are not God's will nor do they come directly from God's hand, but are rooted in creaturely decisions, accidents and chance, and conflict between a static past and an adventurous future. God does not choose the suffering which creatures experience. Still, the contrast between what is and what can be in the adventures of a civilization or cosmos can be painful. To that extent, the presence of conflict and discord in the process of evolution – seen in terms of the quest for justice in human experience

---

15 Whitehead, *Function of Reason*, 15.

– can be disruptive to familiar patterns and the status quo upon which we have come to depend.

The universe is a theater of purpose and creativity working within accident, order, and regularity. A deterministic, mechanistic, and insentient vision of evolution tells only part of our universe, planetary, and civilizational story. Whitehead speculates that "the other side of the evolutionary machinery, the neglected side, is expressed by the word creativeness. The organisms can create their own environment. For this purpose, the single organism is almost helpless. The adequate forces require societies of cooperating organisms. But with such cooperation and in proportion to the effort put forward, the environment has a plasticity which alters the whole ethical aspect of evolution."[16] Competition, and the suffering that emerges from species and groups at cross purposes, exists in the upward trend of evolution. Conversely, cooperation among species and humans is equally important in evolving persons and species.

The great mystery of evolution is the evocation of organisms with fragile survival value like humankind at the mercy of forces beyond us, living in a small physiological comfort zone, and yet able to transform ourselves and the planet to live well and better. Whitehead suggests that our emergence is not just accidental but reflects a restless intentionality, an urge for beauty and intensity of experience. In speaking of the interplay of purpose and chance at the macrocosmic and microcosmic levels, Whitehead observes:

> The material universe has contained in itself, and perhaps still contains, some mysterious impulse for its energy to run upwards. This impulse is veiled from our observation, so far as concerns its general operation. But there must have been some epoch in which the dominant trend was the formation of protons, electrons, molecules, the stars. Today, so far as our observations go, they are decaying. We know more of the animal body,

16 Whitehead, *Science and the Modern World,* 111-112.

through the medium of our personal experience. In the animal body, we can observe the appetition towards the upward trend, with Reason as the selective agency. In the general physical universe, we cannot obtain any direct knowledge of the corresponding agency by which it attained its present stage of available energy.[17]

Just as Teilhard posits the "within" of things, the energy enlivening all creation reflective of the movements of the universal Christ, Whitehead notes the incompleteness of materialistic explanations of evolution. Evolution may not have a final resting point. There may be many futures possible in the ongoing interplay of chance, accident, divine creativity and wisdom, and creaturely decision-making. Still, evolution requires a deeper Eros, an inner passion within each individual reflective of cosmic purpose. The wonder of human life and animal existence, or the scudding of a cloud or revolution of our planet around the sun, require intentionality as well as mechanistic causation.

In contrast to many readings of Teilhard, Whitehead does not invoke a Christ, Omega Point, or a final resting place for evolution. Still, Whitehead, like Teilhard, affirms a persistent arc in the universe toward complexity, intensity, diversity, and beauty that gives birth in the interplay of purpose and chance to a finely tuned planetary environment within which divine purpose can evolve beings like us. Evolution toward complexity and intensity of experience points to the movements of wise creativity, described by Whitehead as "the poet of the world with tender patience leading it by his vision of truth, beauty and goodness."[18] Divine artistry is persistent and, at times, insistent. Love never gives up in the long journey of personal, planetary, and cosmic evolution.

---

17 Whitehead, *Function of Reason*, 24.
18 Whitehead, *Process and Reality*, 346.

3

TEILHARD'S METAPHYSICS OF SPIRITUAL EVOLUTION

God reveals himself everywhere beneath our groping efforts, as a universal milieu, only because he is the ultimate point upon which all realities converge...it is precisely because he is at once so deep and yet so akin to an extensionless point that God is infinitely near, and dispersed everywhere. It is precisely because he is a center that fills the whole sphere.[1]

Pierre Teilhard de Chardin is the theologian of embodiment and evolution. Although he worked with rocks and fossils, Teilhard imaged a personal universe inspired and aiming toward a Personal God. Love makes the world go round. It also propels it forward. Love guides the planets and stars and lures forward the human adventure. Teilhard sought to overcome the tragic dualism that plagued theological dogma and rendered religion irrelevant to the emerging world of science and turned spirituality away from the earth in favor of our heavenly destiny. Beyond binary categories that separate heaven from earth and flesh from spirit is the realm of God on "earth as it is in heaven," honoring embodiment, connection with the non-human world, and affirmation of science and culture. Teilhard believed that we could have communion with the earth, communion with God, and, most significantly, communion with God through discovering God in sacred matter.

---

1   Pierre Teilhard de Chardin, *The Divine Milieu* (New York: Harper and Row, 1957, 114.

Our religious life connects with the totality of our lives. There is no specific religious experience apart from biology, culture, history, and nature. There is no mysticism apart from embodiment. We live in *one, indivisible* world in which the religious vision influences scientific discovery and scientific advances shape our understanding of God and religious experience. Struggling with his vocation to be both priest and scientist, Teilhard realized that we can love God by loving the world and the slow, persistent adventure of evolution. We can affirm the truths of faith and science without conflict or apology. We don't have to choose to embed ourselves in matter or God, we can embrace matter through God and God through matter. The world is ultimately eucharistic.

In the spirit of Carmelite Brother Lawrence's *Practice of the Presence of God,* we can experience God in the eucharistic celebration of the body and blood of Christ. We can also experience the "mass of the world," discovering the holiness of mundane domestic tasks, providing for future generations, crusading for peace and justice, embarking on fossil expeditions, doing laboratory research, charting planetary journeys, and caring for an aging parent. Study and research are prayerful activities whether they involve reflection on scripture, unearthing fossils, or gazing into the Hubble and Webb telescopes.

The God of evolution is present everywhere and in all things, luring the universe forward in part and whole. If whatever we do, we do to God's glory (I Corinthians 10:31), then – as Teilhard asserts – we can be God's companions in "building the earth" and furthering the movements of evolution toward its Omega point, when Christ will be "all in all."

An Evolving Universe. For many Christians, science is the enemy of faith. You can't believe in God and affirm the theory of evolution. Faith depends on the unchanging and unquestioned doctrines and scriptures while science is constantly changing and updating its understanding of reality and human life. In contrast to static concepts of faith, the quest to understand the universe, our planet, and human existence, the scientific adventure is motivated by the motto, *Plus Ultra,* "there is more." Scientists follow the facts regardless of where they lead and even if they challenge previous understandings of reality or their prior achievements. There is more to know about the origins of the universe and the emergence of human life on this planet than we can imagine. There is also more to know about the relationship between humans and their environment, non-human life, and variations in human experience than we can ever encompass.

Contrary to dogmatic thinkers, open-spirited scientists recognize that error is an opportunity for progress in a universe that never stands still. Dogmatic certainty is to be questioned and doctrines are revised in our quest for greater knowledge of ourselves and the world. Deconstruction and chaos may be the womb of new images of God, human life, and the communities of which we are a part. The same spirit of *Plus Ultra* should be true for theological and spiritual adventurers who commit to following the quest for truth and deepening their encounter with God regardless of the consequences to their previous faith positions.

In the Preface, I noted that many Christians believe that their faith is a finished product. They believe that God has nothing new to say beyond the scriptural witness or God's appointed religious leadership and institutions. Infallible scriptures, religious leaders, traditions, and doctrines cannot be questioned. The old-time religion has everything we need spiritually and doctrinally. From this perspective, faith looks backward to primordial perfection, either in the Garden of Eden, the Petrine Rock upon which the church was built, or the infallible and unchanging Holy Scriptures. Although progress occurs in culture and science, traditionalists believe that such change cannot challenge the unchanging truths of faith. When science and faith are in conflict, our hope and trust is in biblical revelation and the authorities of the church and not fallible science.

Christian conservatives fear that questioning doctrines such as the young earth, six-day creation, and original sin threaten the entire edifice of traditional faith, as Teilhard sadly discovered. If we challenge literal – and dare we say, outdated - understandings of the Genesis creation and fall stories, then everything we hold dear is questionable, literal and static understandings of the nature of God, human sin, the incarnation, and the redemptive power of Jesus' cross and resurrection. In a world of change, backward looking traditionalists believe that we must cling to the "old rugged cross" and the "faith of the fathers." Yet, such clinging to the past eventually fails to respond to life in its complexity, technological advances, and the lively movements of history.

Scientific adventurers who tirelessly sought truth, revealed new ways of looking at the universe and saw error as the pathway to greater knowledge, were persecuted, exiled, and even killed by the grand inquisitors of established religion. Ironically, mystics often suffered the same fate, for mysticism drives us beyond doctrine to the experiences from which doctrines emerge. Mystics seek to experience the Living God. Not content with the recipes of faith, stale leftovers from yesterday's religion, but yearning to taste and see God's goodness, they discover that God is often the ultimate iconoclast. Adventurous theologians and scientists assert that our theological reflection is always incomplete and always in process as we seek greater and greater alignment with the universe and the Creative Wisdom that inspires galaxies and the human adventure. For his commitment to truth wherever he found it, Teilhard experienced a type of intellectual martyrdom, enacted by the guardians of orthodoxy who, fearful of his theological creativity, banned publication and public theological lectures for most of his career.

In the twentieth and twenty-first centuries, the battles between faith and science have escalated and have become political as well as religious. The same conflicts that characterized the Scopes Trail in 1925, focusing on teaching of evolution in schools, continue in school boards where the arbiters of faith seek to teach the six day "biblical" creation and young earth as science on par with the contemporary visions of cosmology and evolution. The battle to maintain the one true faith assailed by a scientific and secular world has, in recent years, led to conflicts over wearing of masks, holding worship services, and vaccination during the COVID epidemic.

While conservative and orthodox Christians condemn the scientific adventure whenever it conflicts with their static and authoritarian understanding scripture, doctrine, and ecclesiastical authority, certain science affirming Christian theologians have resolved disputes between faith and science by asserting that faith and science deal with two completely different realities, what has been described by Stephen Jay Gould as "non-overlapping magisteria." Faith deals with values and subjectivity and its descriptions of the world can be seen as metaphorical and mystical. Science deals with facts and the material world. Given the challenges of science, some theologians, seeking to avoid conflict, see science and evolution dealing with parallel but unrelated realities of fact and value, and matter and spirit. In contrast to the subjectivity of religious experience, they believe science strives to be objective in nature. At the end of the day, this perspective creates two unrelated worlds, which never in principle meet in our professional, ethical, and spiritual lives. From this perspective, science has nothing meaningful to do with faith, and our faith has nothing of consequence to share with science. This is detrimental to both religion and science as well as our ability to respond to technological advances related to medicine and artificial intelligence. Religion is marginalized in the modern world and science is often detached from issues of ethics and values.

As we have discovered, Teilhard and Whitehead take a very different path from either conflict or independence in the relationship of science and religion. They affirm that we live in one world, and our science and faith should reflect this unity in which fact and value are interdependent. Teilhard and Whitehead see religion and science in process and growing together in their understanding of reality. While different in emphasis and the locus of authority, religion and science relate to the same realities, influence each other, and grow in relationship to each other's insights and inspirations. Science needs religion to give it heart and values, and to serve as its ethical guide. Religion needs science to address the contemporary world and our evolving understandings of humanity and to expand our horizons of divine creative wisdom. Our concepts of God, human nature, and the diversity of human experience and sexual expression enlarge as we discover a larger universe and a deeper biological and physiological understanding of ourselves. The scientific quest for truth is not a threat to faith but an invitation to a larger vision of God and human existence. We should no more blindly follow the world views of Aristotle and Aquinas than Ptolemy and Newton or Marx or Mao. And, as Whitehead noted, we may discover new ways to understand physics and quantum theory that go beyond Einstein.

In contrast to those who see the scientific adventure as a threat to faith or who separate faith and science to preserve the integrity of both, Teilhard asserts that Christianity is the religion of evolution. The evolutionary movement from simple to complex, and from one celled organisms to culture creating humans, involves not only accident and competition but purpose and love. God in Christ is the heart of matter and the evolutionary process. Without divine guidance and energy, evolution would have stalled long before the emergence of humans. Indeed, for Teilhard, only Christ can animate all things. Evolution is a quest to join complexity, diversity, and unity in which the goal of Wholeness is present in all the parts, luring it forward from the Big Bang to Artificial Intelligence and space travel.

The immense journey from Big Bang to galaxy formation to the creation of stars, solar systems, and planets is the product of Wise Creativity in tandem with chance, accident, and creaturely freedom. Teilhard does not describe the mechanics of divine artistry in cosmogenesis in great detail nor does he articulate the details of God's movements within cells and spirits. Teilhard provides a vision of evolution within which the love and intentionality we find in our human experience is present latently in all things and is a reflection of a Cosmic Love and Intentionality. God's love for the world includes rocks and streams, and amoeba and horseshoe crabs, as well as fetuses and senior adults. Within each creature, God is at work, drawing all things toward fulfillment and unity in Christ-Omega.

In describing the evolutionary journey, scientists assert that the earth was formed approximately 4.6 billion years ago from the dust and gas of planetary and proto-planetary collisions. The emerging planet cooled and gained solidity, and in the process gave birth to oceans and the surrounding atmosphere. Over millions of years simple life forms such as bacteria developed, morphing over approximately 3.5 billion years into more complex flora and fauna, birds and fish, the primordial ancestors of humankind, and eventually *Homo sapiens.* With the rise of humanity, reflecting the reality of evolution come of age, and as humanity evolved, humans became conscious actors not only in their own cultural, scientific, and religious evolution but in the transformation of the planet. Like the evolutionary journey of other creatures, the ascent of humankind occurred through competition and adaptation as well the emergence of an environment favorable to human existence. As bearers of the spirit, humankind evolved by the interplay of choice, struggle, and accident, all shaped by the undercurrent of the Evolving Christ. This does not nullify the wisdom of Genesis 1, which describes a purposive and meaningful universe as "good" or "very good," but never as "perfect," according to my good friend and colleague at Georgetown University Rabbi Harold White. In "goodness," there is possibility for growth and adventure. That which is "perfect" has no room for growth, innovation, or exploration.

To the chagrin of biblical and theological literalists, the theory of evolution is incompatible with dogmatic understandings of creation and original sin. We cannot locate a primordial couple, Adam and Eve. In fact, there may be many "primordial couples," taking the first steps toward conscious decision-making and civilization making. Human life emerged from slow and patient ascent toward consciousness in various continents. We cannot identify the first experiences of pain, suffering, violence, or betrayal, or attribute them to a primordial "original sin." Indeed, as I noted earlier in this text, the experience of suffering – and violent competition – was not brought about by human disobedience of a particular couple but predated human life by millions of years. The reality of suffering is built into the challenges organisms face in securing an environment favorable to their survival and flourishing. The goodness of God's creation is not undermined by the realities of competition, natural selection, competition, or suffering. Moreover, in a God-inspired evolutionary process, the reality of human suffering cannot entirely be attributed to human willfulness. Pain and death characterized the ascent of humankind from the very beginning, long before the mythical Garden of Eden. As evolution comes of age in human experience, we can aim toward justice and beauty and the minimization of suffering, but suffering will still continue as a reflection of our embodiment, mortality, accident, and human self-interest.

To those who hold onto an infallible scripture or church authority, denial of a literal first couple or a primordial fall of humankind, created in the "image of God," jeopardizes the heart of Christianity. Without the doctrine of original sin, they worry that there will be no need for Christ's atonement on the cross. In contrast to traditional theologies of Christ's work in the world, Teilhard asserts that Christ has always been present in the world. Christ as the source of loving evolution was at work long before the appearance of humankind. Christ's purpose in the world is to be the energy and goal of creation, and not merely the sacrifice for sin. The Cross on Calvary reflects God's love in a world of pain and is part of the totality of God's evolutionary work and not its center point. God constantly creates as well as redeems. The ongoing incarnation of God in the evolutionary process provides the context of redemptive suffering and the ultimate quest for wholeness and unity in diversity, in each moment and in the long haul of evolution.

Evolution requires conflict and suffering as well as cooperation. The evocation of higher organisms and the noosphere of planetary intelligence is risky and may lead to the misuse of technology and the carnage of war making. Yet, even here, the God who evolves higher organisms capable of creation and destruction, and love and hate, leads the universe forward by the Energies of Love and the Power of Creative Union.

A Purposive Christ-Inspired Universe. For ages, God has worked "within" all things, providing energy and purpose and guiding them forward from the age of rocks (geosphere) to the age of life (biosphere) to the age of thought (noosphere). Like artists or crafts persons, God works with and within the materials of creation to bring from complex and creative life forms. God has integrated chance and purpose and chaos and order to bring forth humanity, whose task is to consciously become God's companion and fellow artist in building the earth to come, the Christosphere, or Christ-Omega, when Christ will be all in all.

God draws the world forward from within as well as through external relationships. With the emergence of humankind, the biosphere birthed the noosphere, the planetary envelope of consciousness binding together humankind in its diversity. Evolution is unfinished. God's work is unfinished and so is God. Christ is in the making in relationship to creaturely evolution.

Teilhard believes that the noosphere is in the process of evolution as evidenced by the advances in internet, artificial intelligence, and global communication. The world and God in Christ are in symbiotic relationship and are also in the process of becoming and forming a greater world, the realm of Christ Consciousness, in which all life will be united while maintaining its uniqueness. The world is unfinished and so is Christ. Christ will be "all in all," but – and here I may be going beyond a literal reading of Teilhard in some ways – the open-ended character of the Omega point is being created by our day-to-day decisions and commitments.

Divine evolution is an act of love that embraces and transcends accident, competition, chaos, and mechanism on the way

to a personal universe. God loves the world and nurtures it as
a parent would care for a child, sometimes intimately and other
times leaving space for expanded creativity and freedom. God's
dream of all things in Christ inspired divine creativity in particles
and rocks, simple organisms, dinosaurs and mammals, and finally
humankind. Humankind is still a work in progress. We are not
yet fully alive but God is seeking the fully alive human to reflect
divine glory, as second century theologian Irenaeus hoped. In our
self-consciousness, we can build or destroy God's beloved creation.
Yet, evolution persists, as does God, and God's evolutionary goals
will not be defeated, according to Teilhard.

While recognizing the ambiguity of science and technology,
Teilhard believes that the noosphere will eventually evolve toward
the realization of a benevolent and caring planetary consciousness. Every previous stage of evolution will find its fulfillment in
Christ's unification of the noosphere, the envelope of consciousness permeating and enveloping the Earth. The priest-scientist
lives in hope that humankind will abandon power and greed in
favor of loyalty to God's vision of creative unity, complexity, and
community. Teilhard believes that eventually one unified, yet
diverse, humanity will emerge with the passing of nationalism,
and the noosphere itself will evolve into the Christ-Omega, when
humankind discovers its identity as "the light of the world" and
in its complexity, variety, and unity collaborate to bring beauty
to all creation. This is not an eschatological pantheism in which
individual experience is nullified, but a personalizing process in
which our freedom and creativity become fully aligned with God's
creative evolution. Unity inspires differentiation and personalization. The all-encompassing wholeness calls us forward to become
cells in the body of Christ, but even as cells we have our integrity
and personality. Within the Wholeness that draws us forward,
and the Wholeness that is the aim of the universe, God treasures
diversity and freedom, and "makes things make themselves."[2] The
exact nature and time of the realization of the Omega point is

---

2   Teilhard, *Christianity and Evolution*, 82-83

not-predetermined but is shaped by the quality and commitment of our alignment with God's evolutionary vision.

Today, "we see only a reflection [of what we can become], as in a mirror, but then we will see face to face. Now I know only in part; then I will know fully, even as I have been fully known." (I Corinthians 13:12) In the ambiguity of history, there is hope because Christ the Evolver moves within our lives and institutions. The struggle for a new consciousness will be difficult. The forces of individualism, nationalism, and speciesism are strong. But, the magnetic energy of love will prevail. Christ will be "all and all." We look forward to the revelation of who we are becoming and who God is becoming with us. "And now faith, hope, and love remain, these three, and the greatest of these is love." (I Corinthians 13:13)

The Wondrous Within of Things. For Teilhard, evolution is a process of consciousness raising, the gift of the unity of inner energy and outer magnetism. This is a far cry from the dispirited vision of the physical world, promoted by materialist scientists and traditional, supernaturalist theists. The modern world and its materialistic understanding of the world exorcized God, wonder, purpose, and praise from the world and eventually human experience. Christian fundamentalists and scientific materialists alike promoted a mechanistic universe with clear and set laws that dominated both science and ethics. Fundamentalists, drunk on the spirit of Deism despite its apparent denial of the living, acting, and passionate God of history, portrayed God as outside the universe looking in, performing supernatural feats but otherwise uninvolved in our lives. The notion of enchanted woodlands and spirit-inspired creatures threatened the uniqueness of humankind and opened spiritual leadership to Pagan priests, many of whom were women, according to ecclesiastical and fundamentalist theological gatekeepers. The image of divine omnipresence in terms of global revelation and immanence giving birth and guiding the inner spirit of all things threatened ecclesiastical authorities who saw themselves as the only legitimate media of divine revelation and believed that there was no salvation outside of the church and its sacraments. If God was to enter the world at all, traditional religious authorities asserted, God's presence had to occur in terms of an external supernatural act or revelation, transcending creaturely experience and human piety and violating the orderly laws of nature.

Supernaturalism in a mechanistic universe was also invoked to uphold to localize revelation to an infallible scripture and set apart male spiritual authorities and their church. Saving revelation in a mechanistic universe could only appear where God shined God's light in an otherwise dark universe – the bible, the church, the priesthood, the sacraments, and the Christian tradition alone possessed the light of truth in a fallen world.

Ironically, although they eventually banned divine causation entirely, scientific materialists and scientists promoting a mechanistic, clockwork universe, also agreed with their Christian antagonists in maintaining that the physical world was valueless and opaque to any spiritual presence. The non-human world was mute, acting only in terms of stimulus-response, and having no inner passions or values of its own. While traditional theists spoke of this world as God's creation despite its mechanistic structure, both the materialist and traditional theist saw the world as solely as matter in motion and valueless apart from human and divine interests. Apart from angelic beings, human life was the only locus of freedom, creativity, experience, and value.

Human value and sacredness itself were eventually threatened by the growing movement to see human behavior as solely a matter of conditioning or chemical interactions. Again, ironically, the Christian notion of predestination, arising in full force in the modern era among adherents to the Calvinist tradition, saw human behavior and decision-making entirely determined by God. Our salvation and damnation are completely in God's hands in a world in which both catastrophe and good fortune occur as a result of God's good pleasure. Anything outside the predetermined ecclesiastical and doctrinal circle of salvation, including the non-human world and indigenous peoples, was without value and undeserving of ethical consideration.

In contrast, when Teilhard sees the world, he can exclaim "what a wonderful world!" "Love makes the world go round, and love moves the world forward!" Like Whitehead, Teilhard presented an alternative vision of a living, evolving, passionate universe, guided and lured forward by God's inner light. Teilhard describes the nature of reality in terms of the interplay of "within" and "without," which characterizes all creation from the simplest particle to human experience. All creation has an "interior" heart, reflecting the passionate presence of Spirit. While Teilhard does not detail the exact nature of the "within," or God's movements in the "within" our lives and the non-human world, he contrasts it with the "without" or external and stable reality of things and describes the relationship of within and without as that interpenetration of spirit and matter, each of which complements and completes the other. The within and without are one and permeate each other. Matter is inspired and spirit is embodied. Matter is the external face, hiding internal purposes. Spirit is the inner energy of stable matter. Neither matter nor spirit can be separated in our personal experience or the process of evolution. They are two aspects of one reality – spirit, creativity, and action revealed in stability, inheritance, and external appearance. With Walt Whitman, Teilhard can affirm that "all is miracle" because all things bear the image and energy of God. We don't need an external rescue operation or intervention that nullifies human agency and our vocation as God's companions in healing the earth. If we as the human race individually and corporately choose to align ourselves with God's vision of planetary unity, we can respond to the crises we face. God has given us everything we need here on earth in the graceful interdependence of cells, souls, and the human and non-human worlds.

Teilhard, like Whitehead, proclaims an enchanted universe in which there are, to use the language of the Celtic spiritual guides, "thin places," everywhere. "Cleave the wood and I am there," pro-

claims Christ, as reported in the Gospel of Thomas. (77) Look
at any face and you will see God's handiwork in the evolutionary
process! In Teilhard's universe, octopuses have souls and the cells of
our bodies declare God's glory. God, or Christ, is the inner energy
of creation, permeating, and enlivening all things from within and
inspiring them in the without of relationships and evolutionary
progress. The within is the fire and the without is the smoke. The
within is spirit and the without is the fleshly incarnation. Moving from within each creature, God urges evolution forward in
every rock and cell of the universe. The primary, though not only,
earthly carrier and reflection of the goal of the evolutionary process, humankind, reflects the complexity and intensity of experience whose vestiges are present everywhere.

Teilhard knew first-hand the ecstatic praise of the Psalmist.
The interplay of within and without gives birth to a world of praise
and a democracy of revelation in which all creation reveals the passion of Christ-Omega. Like Whitehead, Teilhard describes a world
of praise in which each creature plays its part in the symphony of
evolution. God inspires each creature in concert with God's vision
for all creation. Listen once more, and this time meditatively, to
Psalm 148 in the spirit of divinely guided evolution . And then, if
possible, go for a walk or gaze out your window.

> Praise the Lord!
> Praise the Lord from the heavens;
> praise God in the heights!
> Praise God all his angels;
> praise, all his host!
>
> Praise God , sun and moon;
> praise God, all you shining stars!
> Praise God, you highest heavens
> and you waters above the heavens!

Let them praise the name of the Lord,
for God commanded and they were created.
God established them forever and ever;
God fixed their bounds, which cannot be passed.

Praise the Lord from the earth,
you sea monsters and all deeps,
fire and hail, snow and frost,
stormy wind fulfilling his command!

Mountains and all hills,
fruit trees and all cedars!
Wild animals and all cattle,
creeping things and flying birds!

Kings of the earth and all peoples,
princes and all rulers of the earth!
Young men and women alike,
old and young together!
                    (Psalm 148:1-12, author's paraphrase)

What an amazing world of beauty and praise! The Psalm proclaims that experience and value are coextensive with reality. Although chance, accident, and competition urge forward the evolutionary process, the evolutionary process from the Big Bang to the noosphere reflects an inner eros, urging life forward at every level. Not alone in an unfeeling and mute universe, we are able to join all creation in awareness of Christ moving within us, and then exclaim with flora and fauna, bird and fish, "let everything that breathes, praise God." (Psalm 150:6)

Lively Interdependence. We are connected. An enchanted and evolving universe arises from the interdependence of all things. Relationships are at the heart of a creative universe. To be is to exist in relationship whether we are describing planets revolving around the sun, a cell in our body, the impact of fossil fuels of climate, the emergence of human community and civilization, or the early Christian movement as "the body of Christ." As Teilhard scholar Kathleen Duffy notes, "today, it is clear that matter cannot exist unless it is in interaction. Interdependence, rather than independence, is the hallmark of the cosmos."[3]

We live in a circle of energy in which interdependence and connection aim toward unity, while preserving uniqueness. The ever-evolving tapestry of life is "endless and untearable, so closely woven in one piece that there is not one single knot in it that does not depend on the whole fabric."[4] In awakening to the intricate interdependence of life, we take the first steps to a mystical vision eventuating in a harmonious planet in which humankind "shall beat their swords into plowshares and their spears into pruning hooks; nation shall not lift up sword against nation; neither shall they learn war any more…and we will walk in the light of God." (Isaiah 2:4-5)

Interdependence is the source of unity in diversity, and also diversity in unity, within communities and planetary evolution. Inspired by the interdependence of life, we embrace a new and countercultural vision of ourselves and our Creator. "Once having reached this summit [of perception], you will realize that nothing is isolated, nothing is either small or profane, since the humblest consciousness partially includes the destinies of the universe and cannot improve itself without improving everything around it."[5] In an interdependent universe, history of the world is reflected in every moment of experience and through our creative actions, the future emerges. In the intricate and dynamic interplay of within and without, spirit and matter, we arise from the universe, create with the universe, and give our lives for the universe. Inner cre-

---

3   Kathleen Duffy, SSJ, *Teilhard's Mysticism: Seeing the Inner Face of Evolution* (Maryknoll, NY: Orbis Books, 2014), 46.

4   Pierre Teilhard de Chardin, *Science and Christ* (New York: Harper and Row, 1968), 79.

5   Teilhard de Chardin, *Letters to Two Friends 1926-1952* (New York: New American Library, 1967), 33.

ativity leads to external impact. Self-creation moves forward the evolutionary process.

Seen from the viewpoint of Spirit, we can understand our place in the universe as an energetic particle within the body of Christ, in which our smallest behaviors promote or obstruct the forward movements of personal, communal, and planetary evolution. Well-versed in scripture and especially the writings of the Apostle Paul, Teilhard resonated with Paul's description of the Christian community and, I believe, the cosmos as the body of Christ.

> God has so arranged the body, giving the greater honor to the inferior member, that there may be no dissension within the body, but the members may have the same care for one another. If one member suffers, all suffer together with it; if one member is honored, all rejoice together with it. Now you are the body of Christ and individually members of it. (1 Corinthians 12:25-27)

The interplay of the dynamic unity, interdependence, and diversity reflected in the formation of the universe and each creature, counters the negative movements of entropy and isolated self-interested individualism, that destroy nations and civilizations, and, in contrast to entropy, promote the ultimate well-being of persons and the planet. Although suffering and evil abound due to the quest for survival, accident, and human decisions, the ubiquitous passionate movements of spirit interpenetrating and binding all things together ensure that eventually "all will be well and all will be well, and all manner of things will be well." (Julian of Norwich)

We Matter in Building the Earth. Throughout this text, I have cited the Southern African affirmation of *ubuntu,* "I am because of you, we are because of one another," as representing the reality of interdependence, described by Teilhard and Whitehead. The interplay of agency and interdependence challenges us to become active participants in "building the earth." Although Christ is the

Evolver, luring us forward toward the Omega Point, we are active agents and partners in the process of bringing Christ to birth in our lives and the cosmic process.

While Teilhard does not give a detailed explanation of the relationship of divinity and humanity, and God's role in inspiring our creativity and commitment to evolution, it is clear that humans – and non-humans - are actors in the evolutionary process. Non-humans also play a role in the creative advance of the universe through adapting to and transforming their environment. Yet, although non-humans have experiences, purposes, and values, it is unlikely (although we cannot rule out conscious and intentional planning among non-human animals) that they have a vision of what they and the planet can become as they arc toward the Omega Point. Humans have been described as evolution aware of itself in which our efforts help all creation rise toward its destiny in Christ. In fact, we are the icons of the evolutionary process as we advance from horse and buggy to steam engines and automobiles, airplanes, and rockets, and from speech to writing to the printing press, the computer, and the emergence of artificial intelligence and the dream of planetary unity. We can foster evolutionary growth in the enveloping noosphere. We can create a global village that transcends nationalism and privileges partnership. We can also, by focusing on the devices and desires of our hearts, render the Earth a wasteland uninhabitable for future generations.

Evolution is a dynamic process of call and response in which God calls all creation forward and all creatures have the ability to respond with affirmation, negation, or ambivalence. Over fifty years ago, as a college student, I was inspired by John Cobb's reporting of words from Nikos Kazantzakis' *Report to Greco,* which insightfully describe Teilhard's vision of the evolutionary process:

> Blowing through heaven and earth, and in our hearts and the heart of every living thing, is a gigantic breath – which we call God. Plant life wished to con-

tinue its motionless sleep next to stagnant waters, but the Cry leaped up within it and violently shook its roots: "Away, let go of the earth, walk!" Had the tree been able to think and judge, it would have cried, "I don't want to. What are you urging me to do! You are demanding the impossible!"…It shouted in the way for thousands of eons; and lo! As a result of desire and struggle, life escaped the motionless tree and was liberated.

Animals appeared – worms – making themselves at home in water and mud. "We're just fine here," they said, "We have peace and security; we're not budging."

But the terrible Cry hammered itself pitilessly in their loans, "Leave the mud, stand up, give birth to your betters."

"We don't want to! We can't!"

"You can't, but I can. Stand up!"

And lo! After thousands of eons, man emerged, trembling on his still unsolid legs.

The human being is a centaur; his equine hoofs are planted in the ground, but his body from breast to head is tormented and worked on by the merciless Cry…. Man calls in despair, "Where can I go? I have reached the pinnacle, beyond is the abyss." And the Cry answers, "I am beyond. Stand up!"[6]

God's all-pervasive call, like that of the prophets, John the Baptist, and Jesus, can jar us out of our sense of complacency and call us to earth-evolving action. God calls us forward from within our spirits and in our social interactions to new horizons and to heal and evolve the planet. God's call can be discordant. God challenges static doctrines and backward-looking visions of the universe. But, discord is often the catalyst for creativity and social transformation. One need only think of the abolitionist move-

---

6   Nikos Kazantzakis, *Report to Greco* (New York: Faber & Faber, 1998), 291-292.

ment, the liberation of India, Central and South America, Mexico, and South Africa from colonial rule, the feminist, womanist, and civil rights movements, and Greta Thunberg lecturing her elders on their responsibility to confront global climate change. God calls to creation, seeking creation's companionship, because deep down God needs us to be companions and agents in moving planetary evolution forward. As I noted earlier, for Whitehead and also for Teilhard, God's power is relational, not unilateral. While God has an ultimate goal in history, according to Teilhard, the realization of the Omega Point, the Fullness of Christ, we must be God's co-creators of the noosphere so that the human planetary envelope creates more life rather than destroying the foundations of human and non-human life.

Contrary to orthodox images of omnipotence, in which God can do everything God wishes, both good and evil, on a whim, Teilhard's God is not all-powerful and all-controlling. Nor is the **God of Tomorrow** fully complete. Although the lure of the Omega point is unceasing and universal, God cannot heal and evolve the planet unilaterally. While all things aim toward Christ the Omega as a result of God's Call to the Future, we must align ourselves with the evolutionary arc of the universe to bring God's vision to earth. Christ the Evolver needs partners. Moving within us, Christ elicits our willingness to move from self-interest to world loyalty. The Energy of Love inspires our own loving energy. The divine artisan inspires our own artistry and ingenuity in building the earth and claiming our power in willing relationship to the Reality in whom we live, move, and have our becoming.

Christ the Evolver. Teilhard asserts that only Christ can unite the universe in ways that honor interdependence and individuality. Christ is the Alpha and Omega. Christ motivates the process as Alpha and then, more importantly, guides and energizes the process as Omega. For Teilhard, Christ is the center and goal of all things, whose all-encompassing love is the core energy of the universe. As the prophet Jeremiah affirms, revealing God's intent for Judah and us, "For surely I know the plans I have for you, says the LORD, plans for your welfare and not for harm, to give you a future with hope." (Jeremiah 29:11)

Not restricted to the historical Jesus or confined to human-kind, the Christian tradition, or a particular ecclesiastical body, Christ is God's presence always and everywhere as the guiding energy of evolution. The ultimate reason and purpose of evolution from the Big Bang to the noosphere and the fulfillment of all things is Christ, the love of God incarnate and aiming at fulfilling the deep yearnings of all creation. Christ is within all things and beyond all things, and infinite and intimate. Teilhard's vision of the cosmic and evolving Christ, the one who was, is, and is to be is inspired by three evocative scriptural verses.

Three scriptural insights, significant in the formation of Teilhard's vision of Christ-inspired evolution, provide us with the spiritual lens through which to view the evolutionary process.

Christ is, first of all, the Creative Word and Wisdom of God, the Logos and Sophia, who creates in all things, giving them life and purpose:

> In the beginning was the Word, and the Word was with God, and the Word was God. He was in the beginning with God. All things came into being through him, and without him not one thing came into being. What has come into being in him was life, and the life was the light of all people. The light shines in the darkness, and the darkness did not overtake it…and the Word became flesh and lived among us. (John 1:1-5, 9)

All things bear the divine imprint and come into being and evolve through the Living Word of Christ. Christ's energy – the creating light – enliven and enlighten all things. God's energy of love cannot ultimately be thwarted by human machinations. Even when creatures turn toward darkness, the light still shines within them. Christ "stands at the door and knocks" and rewards those who open to Christ, the vocation of partnership in God's new creation.

Second, the forward movement and ultimate goal of evolution reflect Christ's dynamic creativity. Christ builds the earth along with us, inspiring us to do "greater things" than we can possibly imagine. Christ is also the inner aim or eschaton within each thing and everything.

> He is the image of the invisible God, the firstborn of all creation, for in him all things in heaven and on earth were created, things visible and invisible, whether thrones or dominions or rulers or powers—all things have been created through him and for him. He himself is before all things, and in him all things hold together (Colossians 1:15-17).

The forces of chaos, grounded in our self-interest rather than the affirmation of God's vision of dynamic unity, cannot ultimately prevail. Teilhard believes that rugged individualism will eventually give way to creative interdependence. Christ "holds all things together." Our wonderfully diverse universe of flora and fauna, humankind, and creatures of land and sea, joins unity and diversity. Diversity does not bring division in Christ's evolutionary realm but contributes to God's creative synthesis of all things. Christ is the source of the interplay of Creative Union and Complexity, central to Teilhard's world view.

Third, the Christ to come, embodying the vision of the God of Tomorrow, is the Pleroma, fullness, and plenitude of all things. All things lean toward and are energized by Christ. Yet, Christ is also in process. Christ is evolving along with the universe. Imagine that: Christ is evolving. Just as Jesus grew in wisdom and stature, the impact of Christ in the world is growing and Christ's own energy of love heightens as together we grow closer to planetary wholeness. Christ is present now and also not yet, awaiting full revelation in our lives and the world. The "not-yet God," described by Teilhard scholar Ilia Delio, needs us and grows energetically as a result of commitment to the process of evolution toward the Christ-Omega.[7] Teilhard affirms that we are creating Christ as Christ is creating us. The notion of mutual co-creation bears resemblance to the interplay of God and the world, especially in terms of God's consequent nature in Whitehead's cosmology. "Since Jesus was born, and grew to his full stature, and died, everything has continued to move forward because Christ is not yet fully formed: he has not yet gathered about him the last folds of his robe of flesh and of love which is made up of his faithful followers. The mystical Christ has not yet attained to his full growth; and therefore the same is true of the cosmic Christ. Both of these are simultaneously in the state of being and of becoming."[8]

When all things are subjected to him, then the Son himself will also be subjected to the one who put all things in subjection under him, so that God may be all in all. (1 Corinthians 15:28)

Teilhard's vision of God is profoundly trinitarian. God's dynamic, independent Tri-unity is the model for our own relationships. You can't separate Christ from God the Creator or the Spirit groaning within us in Teilhard's theological vision. If Christ evolves, then God evolves. If Christ needs our companionship to heal the world, then God needs our companionship to heal the world. Nor can you restrict Christ's impact solely to humankind. The Spirit moves in mystical experiences and also the movement joining complexity and unity. Teilhard's trinitarian approach to God in terms of three interdependent persons, united in spirit, is the ultimate symbol of creative and life-giving unity in diversity. Christ's power extends from the birth of the universe to its consummation. The energy of love is present in the creation of galaxies, planets, the formation and evolution of our planet, and the wondrous diversity of the creative process. While Teilhard sees humankind as the pinnacle of Earth's evolutionary process, able consciously to uplift the whole planet in companionship with Christ, human survival and experience are connected with the

---

7   Ilia Delio, *The Not Yet God: Carl Jung, Teilhard de Chardin, and the Relational Whole* (Maryknoll, NY: Orbis Books), 2023.

8   Teilhard, *Hymn of the Universe*, 121.

well-being of the wondrous non-human world. One can assume that if humans have agency and purpose, then at varying degrees there is agency and purpose revealed in the "within" of every creature.

In summary, Christ is the center of all creation, the ultimate principle of evolution, aiming creation toward a Personal Universe with a Personal God. Infinity and intimacy are joined in Christ's ubiquitous incarnation. Not imprisoned in the past, the Alpha undergirds the ever-evolving Omega. Christ the Omega lures, evolves, and grows in relationship to our own evolution. Christ needs our efforts to build the earth and heal creation. In evolving us, Christ also evolves. Christ-Omega is the destiny of all things, but we – humankind and the non-human world – have a significant role in furthering or detracting from God's fulfillment in Christ and in the world. We are, as Teresa of Avila averred, the hands and feed, and heart and mind, of God, and as another Teresa, in our time, asserted, we can do something beautiful for God, we can embody and energize the movements toward Christ-Omega in our lives and the world.

4

A METAPHYSICAL AND SPIRITUAL SYNTHESIS

Chapters Four, Five, and Six comment briefly on the common vision of Whitehead and Teilhard. Like Chapter One, they also present spiritual practices based on a creative synthesis of Teilhard's and Whitehead's vision of metaphysics, mysticism, and mission. Following my description of Whitehead's and Teilhard's unique perspectives, my approach will be to focus on the contours and intentions of their thought and spiritual practice, with only modest regard to areas where they may diverge. My remarks reflect the vision of creative union and complexity, the underlying unity that promotes differentiation, in the universe and also in the interplay of Whitehead's and Teilhard's vision. It is my contention that these parents of contemporary process thought join in common cause to chart a loving, evolving universe, aiming at complexity and creative union, and guided by a personalizing God. Whitehead speaks of the growth of civilization and life in terms of "adventure" and the "teleology of the universe" toward the production of Beauty. Teilhard speaks of the magnetic evolving power of Christ-Omega. In both cases, the power and purpose of God's future vision inspire human partnership. The universe requires our commitment to reach fruition in the moment and over the long haul.

Whitehead and Teilhard are companions in the formation of a new theology to respond to the new world of physics and biology and to reflect the ingenuity, energy, and vision of Tomorrow's God. While we are grateful for our theological and philosophical parents and value tradition, we cannot be content with nor follow without reservations and revisions the theology and philosophy of the past. A new world view calls for new visions of God, theology, spirituality, and ethics. While there are slightly different emphases in their world views and understanding of God's presence and purposes in the evolutionary process, based on their cultural location, religious experience, and scientific orientations, Whitehead and Teilhard fundamentally agree that there is an inner purpose moving through all things, inspiring creative experience in every entity, and that that the universe as a whole is guided toward wholeness, whether we describe this as the Christ-Omega, or the aim at Beauty reflected in the initial aim giving birth to each occasion of experience.

Whitehead and Teilhard posit a living, enchanted universe in which experience and value are coextensive with reality and God works within all things to achieve God's evolutionary vision. Moreover, Christ or God needs our creaturely efforts to achieve God's vision in history and the cosmos. God needs us and evolves along with us. At the human level, and presumably the non-human realm, freedom is real and creatures are able to assist or obstruct the achievement of God's vision. Still, we cannot finally thwart God's vision. Despite our waywardness individually and corporately, God continues to call us forward toward complexity, unity, and intensity of experience to enrich the universe and God's nature.

For Whitehead, there are many possible futures for human life and the universe in response to the moral and spiritual arcs toward beauty. In fact, for Whitehead, there is no final stopping point in the evolutionary adventure. God and the world will continue to grow in relationship to one another in the call and response of life. God aims at beauty, but God's aim at beauty always includes a tragic element. Teilhard is unclear about whether the evolution of the universe into the fullness of being, Christ-Omega, is inevitable or ultimately depends on our alignment with God's vision. Humankind is not fully alive, nor is the universe fully alive. The creation as a whole, as well as in each part, groans in its anticipation of its healing and fulfillment. Teilhard's Omega point must be hyper-personal and hyper-individual as well as unified in Christ. Creative union is joined with personal divinization. Yet, our freedom, though shaped by Christ's aim at wholeness, can further or impede the realization of God's vision for the evolutionary process. As we move toward Omega, the Not-Yet God will evolve toward Wholeness with us. Both Whitehead and Teilhard affirm that God never gives up on the world. Regardless of our decisions, God will continue to lovingly bid us to become companions in transforming the universe. God's love inspires our love, and God's vision or life is not fully realized – "not yet" – until all creation finds wholeness.

Teilhard's overall world view suggests – and here I am going beyond Teilhard's expressed words - that process and agency will continue in the Christ-Omega Point. The Omega Point, like Whitehead's understanding of the relationship of God's "consequent nature" to the world of process is not static but will continue to evolve, I believe, in new, creative, and life-supporting ways. The personalized universe Teilhard envisions must include creativity and freedom and growth both in Christ and us. A completed God, or a static Christ-Omega, as Whitehead and Teilhard recognize, is less alive and personal than a God that constantly and everlastingly interacts in new ways going from "glory to glory." Although Teilhard's Omega Point is, in a sense, complete in an anticipatory way as the fulfillment of evolution, it can no more be static than God is or creaturely experience is static. Perhaps, as scripture suggests, we go from grace to grace, light to light, and glory to glory in an unending community of love:

> And all of us, with unveiled faces, seeing the glory of the Lord as though reflected in a mirror, are being transformed into the same image from one degree of glory to another, for this comes from the Lord, the Spirit (2 Corinthians 3:18).

SPIRITUAL PRACTICES:
LISTENING TO THE VOICES OF EVOLUTION

Whitehead and Teilhard invite us to listen deeply and open our senses to the movements of evolution flowing through our lives and all creation. Evolution reflects the movements of God's moral, spiritual, and incarnational arcs calling the world to new possibilities. The arc of evolution is cosmic and intergalactic. It is also planetary and personal. Planetary evolution – the call of the Omega Point, Christ Consciousness – inspires personal growth in wisdom and stature. Personal spiritual evolution – the movement from self-interest to world loyalty – is essential to planetary evolution and God becoming fully God in the world. We are evolution made conscious of itself and thus able to further hasten the movements of the world toward Greater Beauty and Intensity and to the Universal Christ.

God's evolutionary and spiritual movements in the universe are congruent with God's movements in our lives. Accordingly, we can experience the call of evolution moving through us and align ourselves with the evolutionary process toward Christ Being All in All. In aligning ourselves with God's movements within us, we discover God in all things, the energy of love enlivening all things, and experience and value in all things. We discover our vocation as earth builders and healers. The world is saved one moment at a time and each moment can further the arc of spiritual evolution in our world.

Listening to Creation. In this spiritual exercise, begin with a time of quiet, simply breathing deeply the energy of the universe, the breath of life, letting it fill and connect you with the God-filled universe around and within you. Feel the spiritual and moral arcs, the Christ Consciousness, flowing in and through you as your deepest reality, coaxing you toward greater freedom and creativity individually and relationally.

In the stillness of unity with all creation, ask God to reveal your vocation in moving the arcs of evolution, spirituality, and morality forward. Experience yourself as a companion with God in evolving the world as you listen for God's guidance.

Throughout the day, be attentive to the movements of God in your life and your various responsibilities and roles, encounter by encounter, in healing and evolving the Earth. Make a commitment to be God's companion in healing the earth.

Sheer Delight. Whitehead notes that "enjoyment" is at the heart of experience. Enjoyment emerges from the interplay of environment and intentionality. Moreover, as I noted earlier in this chapter, Whitehead avers that "the world beyond is so intimately entwined in our own natures that unconsciously we identify our more vivid experiences with it." Spirituality involves deep intentionality and focus, for example, in praying the hours or the use of mantras or prayer words in meditation. Spirituality may also involve the sheer enjoyment of being, opening our senses to the world around us, and accepting the graceful interdependence of life as it enters our experience. In opening to the world, we experience the fire within and without of which Teilhard speaks. In this exercise, simply pause, take time to read Psalm 148, quoted earlier in this chapter, and notice the beauty around you.

Delight in your body and the sights around you. If you are walking, enjoy the process of moving and the changing environment around you. Delighting in the universe, experience a spiritual kinship with the singers of the Navajo Blessing Prayer:

> In beauty I walk
> With beauty before me I walk
> With beauty behind me I walk
> With beauty above me I walk
> With beauty around me I walk
> It has become beauty again.

See Beauty in all things and in the process bring Beauty to all things.

5

WE ARE ALL MYSTICS

*If you would like to phrase it so, philosophy is mystical.
For mysticism is insight into depths as yet unspoken. But
the purpose of philosophy is to rationalize mysticism; not by
explaining it away, but by the introduction of novel verbal
characterizations, rationally coordinated... The world lives
by the incarnation of God in itself.[1]*

*I am a child of the Earth before being a child of God.
I only can grasp the divine through the Cosmic. You will
never understand if you do not see that.[2]*

Whitehead and Teilhard recognize that deep down, we are
all mystics. Divine energy and inspiration are constantly flowing through our lives. But, most of the time, we don't know it.
Teilhard and Whitehead affirm that we live in a God-filled universe. God's vision of possibility gives birth to each moment of
experience and guides the cosmic adventure. God is the energy
love or eros that animates the "within" of all creation and sparks
the self-creation of each occasion of experience. There is, as the
Hebraic patriarch Jacob discovers, a ladder of angels everywhere.
Every so often, we move from our typical experience, "God was
in this place – and I did not know it" to "God is in this place –
and I now I know." Such moments illuminate the totality of life
– whether sought after, unbidden, or through near death experiences – enabling us, with psychiatrist Carl Jung, to say that we not
only believe in God, "we know." The great religions of the world

---

1   Whitehead, *Modes of Thought*, 174 and *Religion in the Making*, 149
2   Pierre de Chardin, *Lettres À Jeanne Mortier*, 58-59.*

have their birth in mystic encounters with God as our deepest self, the energy of love moving through all things, the source of possibility, the moral and spiritual arc, the personal and transpersonal reality, "in whom we live and move and have our being." (Acts 17:28) Open your senses and spirit and you will discover the divine in yourself and in all things and feel the movements of evolution flowing through you.

Like the experience of falling in love, mystical experiences are almost impossible to define and describe. Mysticism is many faceted and although the mystic recognizes the Holy as beyond all finite description, the Holy also appears as alive in our concrete experiences and the world in which we live. Simply put, mysticism is the encounter with the Ultimate Reality, or what I describe as "the Holy Adventure", that gives birth to and guides our lives and the universe. It is the encounter with the Infinite in our very finite experiences as timely mortals, in which this moment – and every moment – becomes a "thin place," as the Celtic Christians proclaim, transparent to divinity. Every moment becomes an incarnation of Creative Wisdom, whether revealed as the ever-flowing Tao, the Christ within, the Buddha nature, the Eternal Self, or the Great Spirit of First American spirit guides. Although our words differ and never fully capture the divine, in mystical experiences, the world comes alive, the stress of isolated individuality is relieved, and we experience the peace that passes all understanding.

Like Jesus' Transfiguration on the Mountaintop, mystical experiences are unique to this moment in time and yet enlighten and enliven the rest of our lives. Our senses open, our hearts come alive, and we experience the world in all its tragic beauty as Holy and Beloved with a peace that illumines and surpasses our individual personality and perspective. Our mystical experiences may even contribute to the evolution of the universe, as Teilhard suggests.

Annie Dillard unexpectedly experiences the Holy on a walk in the woods, and her whole life is transfigured. According to the author of *A Pilgrim at Tinker Creek*:

> One day I was walking along Tinker Creek thinking of nothing at all and I saw the tree with the lights in it. I saw the backyard cedar where the mourning doves roost charged and transfigured, each cell buzzing with flame. I stood on the grass with the lights in it, grass that was wholly fire, utterly focused and utterly dreamed. It was less like seeing than like being for the first time seen, knocked breathless by a powerful glance. The lights of the fire abated, but I'm still spending the power. Gradually the lights went out in the cedar, the colors died, the cells unflamed and disappeared. I was still ringing. I had my whole life been a bell, and never knew it until at that moment I was lifted and struck. I have since only rarely seen the tree with the lights in it. The vision comes and goes, mostly goes, but I live for it, for the moment when the mountains open and a new light roars in spate through the crack, and the mountains slam.....[3]

Dillard discovers with Teilhard the gleaming presence, the glow of the Holy, illuminating all things. The within is without, and without is within.

Religion, as Whitehead says, involves solitude and privacy that inspires self-transcendence. Our unique encounter with divinity resonates with the whole universe. Mystical experiences can also occur in the hustle and bustle of a city street as Thomas Merton discovered in downtown Louisville, Kentucky. On a rare outing from Gethsemani,

> ...at the corner of Fourth and Walnut, in the center of the shopping district, I was suddenly overwhelmed with the realization that I loved all those people, that

---

3 Annie Dillard, *Pilgrim at Tinker Creek* (New York: Harper, 1984), 45.

they were mine and I was theirs, that we could not be
alien to one another even though we were total strangers.

It was like waking from a dream of separateness...
The whole illusion of separate holy existence is a dream.[4]

We may practice contemplation and asceticism for years and
eventually experience Enlightenment as Gautama did while meditating under the Bodhi Tree. We may also experience the Holy
Spirit descending as a dove to bless and anoint Jesus following
his baptism at River Jordan or in the flames and winds of Pente-
cost, embracing all the colors of the rainbow and races of humankind. Whether mystical experiences are gradual or unexpected,
we are forever changed by the reality that has been our previously
unknown companion. For both Whitehead and Teilhard, mystical experiences illuminate depths unspoken, and yet they arise
from that which is present everywhere as our deepest reality and
the deepest reality, the energy of love and the poet of the universe,
present in all things and inspiring the arcs of personal and cosmic
evolution.

The mysticism of Whitehead and Teilhard is profoundly *kat-
aphatic,* reflected in our encounters with God in the embodied
world of the senses. The heavens truly declare God's glory and
we can taste and see divinity. All things are words of God, as the
German mystic Meister Eckhart averred. Rocks contain angels, as
Teilhard discovered. The "within" of life shines forth and can be
named. Yet, Teilhard and Whitehead also appeal to the dazzling
darkness that gives birth to the *apophatic* faith which recognizes
that God is always "more" than we can describe or imagine. The
Deep Mystery of God lures us forward and challenges any attempt
to localize God – or limit God – to any doctrine, institution, or
religious tradition. In that spirit, Teilhard and Whitehead recognized their limitations as students of religious experience: although

---

4   Thomas Merton, *Essential Writings,* edited by Christine M. Bochen
     (Maryknoll, NY: Orbis Books), 90

they were aware of and affirmed the gifts of other religious traditions, their framework was Christian, theologically and spiritually.

While focus on a particular tradition's wisdom is essential both in theological and spiritual formation, there is always something important gained from immersing yourself in the world's spiritual traditions. Whitehead and Teilhard were aware of the multiplicity of religious traditions, but they were also persons of their times, living before the migration of Asian religious traditions to the West and the recognition of the insights of African, Celtic, First American, earth-based, and indigenous spiritualities. Although they mentioned other faith traditions in their writings, I am sure that if they were living today they would have more fully welcomed serious encounters with theologians and spiritual leaders of other faiths and would have seen significant benefits in the inter-spirituality or dual participation that characterizes the experiences of many spiritual seekers, including my own Christian affirmation of Taoism, Hinduism, and Japanese healing techniques as central to my spirituality.

In the paragraphs ahead, I will reflect on the relationship of metaphysics and mysticism in the work of Whitehead and Teilhard and then invite you to awaken to your inner mystic and the Creative Wisdom "in which you live and move and have your being." (Acts 17:28) In awakening to the divine "within," we may experience God "without," and discover our vocation as contemplative activists, living out our mission as participants in global evolution.

WHITEHEAD'S METAPHYSICAL MYSTICISM

"Deep down, we are all mystics," the title of this chapter, may initially seem innocuous but this affirmation is controversial and prophetic. If we are all mystics, and mysticism reveals the deepest nature of reality, then everyone has a portal to divinity, and, regardless of class, age, race, sexuality, nation of origin, or neurological status, we can experience the Holy and become vehicles of revelation. Although he never claimed to be a mystic and made only a handful of comments directly related to mysticism, Whitehead was steeped in theology and, I suspect, the history of mysticism, and was appreciative of the impact of Buddhism as a world religion. Whitehead's work charts a democracy of revelation, like Francis of Assisi's and Teilhard's, that is often at odds with the proponents of authoritarian, backward looking, dogmatic and static religion. In addition to containing profound insights into the nature of reality, I believe that Whitehead's *Process and Reality*, *Adventures of Ideas*, *Modes of Thought*, *Science and the Modern World*, and *Religion in the Making* can be seen as invitations to mysticism.

The World Lives by Incarnation of God. For Whitehead, God can be found in every moment of experience. Each moment of experience arises from the symbiosis of its immediate environment, the universe at large, and God's vision for this moment in time. Whitehead uses the term *initial aim* to describe God's creative wisdom and presence as the catalyst for each moment of experience. The initial aim is the energy of possibility that gives birth to and orients each moment of experience. God's aim within each occasion provides the appropriate blend of order and novelty . For each moment of experience and its immediate future, the process of self-creation is dependent on the complexity and potential impact on its particular environment. God's vision for each entity, from the energy of a quantum particle to the compassion of a loving parent or insights of an ecstatic mystic, is for fulfillment in the present moment and positive impact on the future. Contextual in nature, God's aims for higher organisms – and even "primitive" occasions of experience - are never abstract and unrelated to our personal context, history, and hopes. Some version of God's aim toward wholeness or intensity is present everywhere in accordance with the unique setting in which an occasion of experience arises.

God's aim is relational and not coercive. God's power in the universe involves, especially in human experience, the presentation of ideals to elicit creative freedom and relationality. According to Whitehead, "God in the world is the perpetual vision of the road which leads to deeper realities."[5]

Whitehead asserts that freedom is real at every level of life, including the quantum and cellular levels. Chaos and accident occur: cells grow in ways that threaten the organisms within which they exist; cars careen on icy pavement; buildings collapse leaving persons homeless and killing residents; political leaders set in motion processes that lead to war. Humans turn from the moral and spiritual arcs of the universe, choosing self-interest over concern for the environment; using power to destroy faith in democracy and threaten civil society; putting success over family life, integrity, and planetary survival. Still, God persists as the inner eros, the voice of conscience, inviting us to embody the "better angels of our nature." In language that joins metaphysics and mysticism, Whitehead affirms that God's

> Purpose in the world is quality of attainment. God's purpose is always embodied in the particular ideals relevant to the actual state of the world. Thus all attainment is immortal in that it fashions the actual ideals which are God in the world as it is now. Every act leaves the world with a deeper or a fainter impress of God. He then passes into his next relation with the world with enlarged, or diminished, presentation of ideal values.[6]

What we do, our actions and values, makes a difference to God and promotes healing or destruction, and life or death, in the world. Recognizing the intimacy of our relationship with God, the mystic seeks to intuit God's vision for this moment in time. Indeed, a Whiteheadian mysticism "hears" the voice of God and experiences the divine intentionality for our lives. In traditional religious language, mysticism is a matter of "vocation" or call. Isaiah experiences God's presence filling the whole earth. His spirit is stirred by angelic voices chanting that "the whole earth is filled

5   Whitehead, *Religion in the Making,* 151.
6   Ibid., 152.

with God's glory" and then hears the deeper call of the Spirit, "Whom shall I send?" and responds "Here I am send me." (Isaiah 6:1-8) God asks the same question of us: how will we join our inner religious experiences with God's call to heal the Earth?

Whitehead would have endorsed psychiatrist Carl Jung's quote from Erasmus, posted on the door to his Zurich home, "Bidden or unbidden God is present." God is here and when the doors of perception are cleansed, we realize that we always stand on Holy Ground, whether in an ashram, sanctuary, study, kitchen, laboratory, or playground.

Awakened to divine possibility in each moment of experience and encounter, the mystic aims to embody the values of truth, beauty, and goodness, to see the light and then be the light, illuminating the world around them. (Matthew 5:13-16) As we will see in the next chapter, metaphysics and mysticism are intimately connected with our personal and political mission and our calling to save and build the earth. The mystic experiences holiness in all things – an essential "rightness" moving through reality - and desires to "do something beautiful for God," as Mother (Saint) Teresa counsels, in response to God's presence "in the least of these." This "beautiful" act can inspire us to individual compassion or political action for the good of the whole.

In words can be both invitational and chilling, Whitehead asserts that "God's aim is the best for that impasse. But if the best be bad, then the ruthlessness of God can be personified as Atè, the goddess of mischief."[7] For just such a time as this, our calling is to open the door to a greater influx of divine possibility by a commitment to world loyalty and openness to personal and global wellbeing. This can mean harmony. It can also mean discord to those who hold onto the status quo of static religion and promote authoritarian politics. We may be agents of peace and harmony and also wield the non-violent sword of the spirit challenging dead doctrines and dangerous theologies as well as the abuse of religion for power and political gain.

---

7   Whitehead, *Process and Reality,* 244.

The world lives by the incarnation of God, and we are expressions of God's incarnational vision, according to Whitehead. Moment by moment "new mercies we see," as the hymn "Great is Thy Faithfulness" proclaims. With each breath, God comes to us, inspiring and challenging us to fulfill God's vision through our personal decisions each moment of the day. God's incarnation is personal and unique, and institutional and seasonal, constantly evolving as we grow from infant to elder, constantly calling us forward to larger dimensions of selfhood and sacrifice for the healing and evolution of our communities and the world. While often we are oblivious to God's presence in our lives and the world, the mystic experiences God's aim, or vision, in their life and out of that experience, envisions God's presence in all creation.

God Comes to Us in All Things. According to Whitehead, God enlightens and enlivens each moment of our experience, even when we are unaware of God's deep-down and all-pervasive presence. This divine incarnation applies to our personal experience and everything we encounter. Whitehead describes a God filled universe in which God's vision or aim is for intensity of experience in the present moment and for the relevant future. God's aim is never individualistic or solitary, although it addresses each individual moment of experience as it arises. God calls us to be artists and poets of experience whose spiritual artistry is aimed at supporting the wellbeing of those around us. Conversely, the divine comes to us through others in every encounter. "The heavens declare the glory of God" and God also addresses us in our neighbor's words and experiences. God may be speaking to us through God's inspiration of others. There are, as the Celtic spiritual guides say, thin places everywhere. To recapitulate the words of Maltbie Babcock:

> This is my Father's world,
> The birds their carols raise,
> The morning light, the lily white,
> Declare their maker's praise.
> This is my Father's world,

He shines in all that's fair;
In the rustling grass I hear Him pass;
He speaks to me everywhere.

"God speaks to us everywhere."   Nineteen hundred years
before Babcock penned "This is My Father's World," the Gospel of
John asserts, "The true light which enlightens everyone was coming into the world." (John 1:9) and the non-canonical yet equally
revelatory Gospel of Thomas (77) reports Jesus saying:

> I am the light which is on them all. I am the All, and
> the All has gone out from me and the All has come back
> to me. Cleave the wood: I am there; lift the stone and
> thou shalt find me there!

God speaks to us through the human and non-human world.
Every encounter points to the hidden, and often unbidden, movements of God. Whether we describe the mystical experiences of a
Celtic monk, indigenous spiritual guide, Zen monk, Taoist way-
farer, or a fellow shopper at the market, mystics live in a world in
which we can receive divine messages in every encounter. God
encounters us in every face and word, even those which we perceive as misguided. "There is something of God" to be discerned
in others, for those who look deeply in the face of a January 6
insurrectionist, undocumented worker, neuro-divergent school
child, as well as in the successful honor roll student, Trappist
monk, or Hindu rishi. "God in all things," reflecting the spirit
of panentheism, alerts us to the holiness of every creature and the
potential of each creature to illuminate our spiritual journey. "All
things in God" awakens us to the importance of ordinary actions
and our role in shaping the world around us.

The Solitary and Social Nature of Mysticism. Although Whitehead is often cited as the philosopher of interdependence, his best-
known description of religion is "what an individual does with
[their] solitariness."[8] We can experience God in the heart of the

---

8   Whitehead, *Religion in the Making,* 16.

city and in worship services. Yet, in solitude, we experience the congruence between our deepest intuitions and God's presence in our lives and the world. Whitehead notes that the great religions of the world have their origins in solitary moments – Jesus tempted in the wilderness, Buddha meditating, Mohammed hearing the voices of Allah in the cave. These solitary moments give birth to "the small selection" of experiences which become the lens through which we interpret reality and gain a transcendent vision through which to navigate our uncertain and conflictual world.[9] Quiet moments of self-transcendence awaken us to our true spiritual stature as reflections of divine wisdom or manifestations of the Tao, and transfer our attention from individual aggrandizement to world loyalty. Experiencing our spiritual center in solitude connects us with the spiritual centers of our neighbors and opens our attention to the expanding spiral of divine presence in the human and non-human world. Individual enlightenment becomes the catalyst for world loyalty and prophetic faith, as we see in the Buddhist Bodhisattva and the prophets Isaiah and Amos.

Mysticism and Prophetic Faith. Mysticism widens the self to identify with the world beyond us and a future extending far beyond our lifetimes. Jesus "grew in wisdom and stature." The mystic's self-transcendence leads to overcoming fear and alienation of otherness. Even awaiting our deaths, as Francis of Assisi proclaims in his *Canticle of the Creatures,* our experiences can become a portal into divinity and an occasion for praise. In fact, there is no "other" in an interdependent universe. We are all connected and depend on each other for our wellbeing. *Ubuntu,* "I am because of you. We are because of one another." One of the most influential interpreters of Whitehead, Bernard Loomer, speaks words well worth repeating, words that have guided my own theological reflection and political involvement, descriptive of mystical self-transcendence in terms of "S-I-Z-E" or stature:

---

9   Ibid., 31.

By size I mean the stature of a person's soul, the
range and depth of his love, his capacity for relationships. I mean the volume of life you can take into your
being and still maintain your integrity and individuality,
the intensity and variety of outlook you can entertain
in the unity of your being without feeling defensive or
insecure. I mean the strength of your spirit to encourage
others to become freer in the development of their diversity and uniqueness.[10]

While we will discuss the social and political nature of
Whitehead's and Teilhard's thought in the next chapter, Whitehead believes that the nature of mysticism – and all self-creation,
at its best - is incarnational and not escapist. Awakened to the
ubiquitous presence of God, we plunge into the maelstrom of life.
Whitehead notes that there is no specific and separate religious
experience, abstracted from ordinary life. Rather, our religious
experiences emerge from our encounters with the world around us
and within us. Holistic and incarnational in nature, our encounters with God provoke a "world consciousness" in which we seek
to imitate God's own love for the world. Aligning ourselves with
God's aims in our lives, we join our self-realization with the apotheosis of the universe, challenging everything that stands in the
way of persons experiencing the fulfillment that comes from our
encounters with God. Mysticism leads to mission, the prophetic
consciousness in which we seek to preserve and enhance the
intrinsic value of reality and join God in building the earth. From
the solitude of meditation comes the activism of world transformation.

---

10 Bernard Loomer, "S-I-Z-E is the Measure," Henry James Cargas and
   Bernard Lee, *Religious Experiences and Process Theology* (Mahweh, NJ:
   Paulist Press, 1976), 70.

TEILHARD'S EVOLUTIONARY MYSTICISM

Teilhard's biographer Ursula King describes Teilhard as "a great contemporary Christian mystic in the best tradition of Christian mysticism, but also a mystic in search of a new mystical way, a new spirituality open to the rhythm of the contemporary world and its ongoing development."[11] Teilhard's mystic vision joined heaven and earth. He believed that persons could commune with God through the earth. We can find God in the fossil field and through contemplative prayer. When we lack bread and wine for the eucharist, we can say mass over the gleaming, blazing, and evolving world. God is known in the breaking bread. We can also experience Emmaus insights in intimate spiritual relationships, as Teilhard did, and in the seasons of the year. Divinity is found in rocks and also worship services.

Teilhard the Mystic. Teilhard was a cradle mystic, raised by a father who prided himself as an amateur natural historian and a mother for whom the mystics of Christianity and the sacred heart of Jesus were daily companions. Teilhard's life as a scientist-priest can be interpreted as the creative synthesis of his parents' spiritual and intellectual vocations. Early on Teilhard discovered that he didn't need to choose between God and the world, but could love God in the world of rocks, fossils, meadows, and meadows and trees. Inspired by Jesus, who loved the birds of the air and lilies of the field, Teilhard affirmed that the scientific quest to understand the world God loved was an act of faith.

As he wandered the hills and fields of Auvergne, young Teilhard had his first glimpses of what Annie Dillard described as the "tree with lights." As a child and youth, he experienced what he described as "the crimson glow of matter" and "the divine radiating from the depths of matter."[12] Teilhard recalls that as a child he was

---

11 Pierre Teilhard de Chardin and Ursula King, *Pierre Teilhard De Chardin: Writings*, Modern Spiritual Masters Series (Maryknoll, NY: Orbis Books, 1999), 20.

12 Pierre Teilhard de Chardin, *The Heart of Matter* (London: Collins, 1978), 16. Passage translated by Ursula King.

troubled by life's perpetual perishing. When his mother trimmed a few curls from his hair, the child Teilhard, perhaps five or six, held them near to a fire and they were incinerated in less than a second. Recalling that childhood experience, Teilhard notes, "a terrible grief assailed me. I had learned that I was perishable."[13] Teilhard commentator Ursula King notes that Teilhard's love of stones and eventually the science of stones, geology, flowed from his quest for something permanent in a world of flux.   Later he was to experience the faithfulness of Christ the Evolver, the Living Word of God, who joins the everlasting love with the ever-evolving world.

Throughout his life as priest and scientist Teilhard sought to experience God in the quotidian moments of life and in the eternal verities present in a constantly evolving universe. Teilhard experienced his personal vocation as priest in wartime as part of a larger cosmic vocation in which each person and all creation can further God's vision. Amid the carnage of World War I, we can realize that the "true summons of the cosmos is a call consciously to share in the great work that goes within it."[14]   Going within contemplatively in times of war and crisis, Teilhard found that God was also present in the events of human history and the evolution of the planet, and that our relationships and scientific commitments are portals to divinity.

Teilhard championed a sensate mysticism. A North African Desert Parent once stated that the monk is all eye. Teilhard would agree and go beyond this description of monastic life as visual. The monk, like the mystic and scientist, embraces the senses and sees the world as an icon of divine creativity. "It is essential to see things as they are and to see them really and intensely."[15] In the spirit of Plato, the beauty we see in the world of rocks, flora and fauna, and animal life, not to mention the human face, inspires

---

13 Claude Ceunot, *Teilhard de Chardin: A Biographical Study* (London: Burns and Oates, 1965), 3.

14 Pierre Teilhard de Chardin, *Writings in Time of War* (London: Collins, 1968), 32

15 Teilhard de Chardin, *The Divine Milieu*, 58.

us to see the inner beauty of life in its totality as well as the particular expressions with which we are familiar. The external beauty is a pathway to God, and not an illusion to be overcome. Christ comes to us in the world of the flesh, through all our senses, and Christ also points to God's realm within all creation. The trained eye can discover the passionate Spirit moving through the "within" of things. Like the rough-hewn geode, the outer shell is the invitation to explore the wonders within. Teilhard sought "to see God everywhere…in all that is most hidden, most solid, and most ultimate in the world."[16]

Teilhard's eucharistic spirituality went far beyond the exclusivism of the Roman Catholic mass to awaken our perception of the body of Christ in all things and the blood in the Christ in the sufferings attending the evolutionary process. Although he lamented the banning of his writing, and the spiritually deadening teachings of the Roman Catholic ecclesiastical leadership, Teilhard's sense of sacred matter and divine evolution could not be stifled. Pondering Teilhard's indefatigable spirit, despite the ecclesiastical persecution he experienced, I was reminded of the nineteenth century American hymn, "How Can I Keep from Singing":

> My life flows on in endless song;
> Above earth's lamentation,
> I catch the sweet, tho' far-off hymn
> That hails a new creation;
> Thro' all the tumult and the strife
> I hear the music ringing;
> It finds an echo in my soul—
> How can I keep from singing?
>
> What tho' my joys and comforts die?
> The Lord my Saviour liveth;
> What tho' the darkness gather round?
> Songs in the night he giveth.

---

16 Ibid., 46.

No storm can shake my inmost calm
  While to that refuge clinging;
  Since Christ is Lord of heaven and earth,
  How can I keep from singing?

I am sure that Teilhard, the theological martyr (in the sense that the established church banned the publication of his work during his lifetime) would have resonated with additional lyrics, penned by Doris Plenn in 1950, during the final years of Teilhard's life, and identified with the courage of those who kept the faith in the context of political persecution in the United States following World War II.

When tyrants tremble, sick with fear,
And hear their death-knell ringing,
When friends rejoice both far and near,
  How can I keep from singing?
In prison cell and dungeon vile,
  Our thoughts to them go winging;
When friends by shame are undefiled,
  How can I keep from singing?

Teilhard's ecclesiastical persecutors are gone, footnotes in an evolving universe. Freed from the captivity of backward-looking dogma and authoritarian ecclesiastical power, Teilhard's words live on, giving hope for those who seek to embody God's great work in our time. How can we keep from singing for God is near and God's truth and evolving love flow on, despite our clinging to the past or the persecutions we face. In his final years, Teilhard confided in his friend and fellow Jesuit Pierre Leroy, "I really feel that now I am always living in God's presence."[17]

The presence of God in the world and in the scientific adventure inspired Teilhard to propose a new mysticism to companion

---

17 Mary Lucas and Ellen Lucas, *Teilhard* (Garden City, NY: Doubleday, 1977), 339.

the new theological vision necessary for the survival of Christianity and, quite possibly, the planet:

> We need a new theology and a new approach to perfection, which must be gradually worked out in our houses of study and retreat houses, in order to meet the new needs and aspirations. . . . But what we need perhaps even more . . . is for a new and higher form of worship to be gradually disclosed by Christian thought and prayer, adapted to the needs of tomorrow's believers without exception.[18]

Embracing the Within of All Creation. Teilhard proclaimed the deep "within" of things as the home of divine passion. Whether particle, rock, or animal, there is an inner fire that gleams in all creation. Similar to Quaker spirituality, Teilhard believed that all things have inner light, and something of God within them.

Teilhard lived in hope of a "new Francis." Perhaps, he was the one he was hoping for in his discovery and message of the "spirit of fire" in all things. The "within" of creation awakens us to holy vision. Nothing is foreign. Nothing is other. Nothing is God-forsaken. We live in a God-filled world in which all things, as Meister Eckhard affirmed, are "words of God." There is no room for world-denying asceticism in Teilhard's theology. Although we may fast and pray, our spiritual practices are aimed at tuning our inner and outer senses to God's revelation in all things. The democracy of revelation described in Psalm 148 and in Teilhard's Christ-inspired universe is also revealed in Francis of Assisi's *Canticle of the Creatures.* Assailed by declining health and facing his mortality, Francis of Assisi sang a hymn of praise to God revealed in every moment and every creature.

> Be praised, my Lord, through all your creatures,
> especially through my lord Brother Sun,
> who brings the day; and you give light through him.

---

18 Teilhard, *Science and Christ* (London: Collins, 1968), 220.

And he is beautiful and radiant in all his splendor!
Of you, Most High, he bears the likeness.

Praise be You, my Lord, through Sister Moon
and the stars, in heaven you formed them
clear and precious and beautiful.

Praised be You, my Lord, through Brother Wind,
and through the air, cloudy and serene,
and every kind of weather through which
You give sustenance to Your creatures.

Praised be You, my Lord, through Sister Water,
whichis very useful and humble and precious and chaste.

Praised be You, my Lord, through Brother Fire,
through whom you light the night and he is beautiful
and playful and robust and strong.

Praised be You, my Lord, through Sister Mother Earth,
who sustains us and governs us and who produces
varied fruits with colored flowers and herbs....
Praised be You, my God, through our sister Bodily Death,
from whom no one can escape.

Praise and bless my Lord,
and give Him thanks
and serve Him with great humility.[19]

Inspired by the Teilhard's vision of a God-filled universe and anticipation of a new Francis, we can chant doxologically with all creation, "Let everything that breathes, praise God" (Psalm 150:6)

---

19 Murray Bodo, *Francis: The Journey and the Dream* (Cincinnati, OH: Franciscan Media, 2011), 169-170.

and perhaps discover that we are also the "new Francis" for which we and the world have been waiting.

A Mysticism of Relational Becoming. Like Whitehead, Teilhard affirms a mysticism of becoming. Each creature arises from, reflects, and contributes to the history of the universe. Even on spiritual retreat, we are connected to the mystics and saints of the church, Christ's first followers, the prophets, and Jesus himself. Our personal interior life – our "within" – is connected by both history and divine intentionality with every other "within." Christ is the binding force of evolution who holds all things together in their process of becoming and impact on the future.

Teilhard's mystical vision undergirds our personal relationships and social responsibility. A decade after Teilhard's death, Martin Luther King articulated a spirituality of social activism.

> It all boils down to this, that all life is interrelated. We are caught in an inescapable network of mutuality, tied into a single garment of destiny. Whatever affects onedirectly, affects all indirectly. We are made to live together because of the interrelated structure of reality.[20]

Despite our temptation to prize rugged individualism and believe that we can go it alone, we are all connected by Christ's evolutionary love incarnate in Christ's body, the evolving universe. No nation, community, species, race, and individual can go it alone. We need one another to flourish as nations and persons, and in the spirit of Teilhard, to further the evolutionary adventure, as King asserts: "For some strange reason I cannot be what I ought to be until you are what you ought to be. And you can never be what you ought to be until I am what I ought to be. That's the way God's universe is made."[21]

---

20 Martin Luther King, Jr. *Testament of Hope: The Essential Writings and Speeches of Martin Luther King, Jr.* (edited by James M. Washington), (New York: HarperSanFrancisco, 1986), 254.
21 Martin Luther King, Jr., *A Knock at Midnight* (New York: Warner Books), 208.

Mystics feel the heartbeat of God in all things and see them-selves as kin with all creation. Teilhard's vision of mysticism expands our empathy and sense of gratitude to include the past evolutionary journey of single celled organisms, dinosaurs, and proto-humans and honor our current and future companions in the adventure toward the full realization of the noosphere, the Christosphere. In this moment of time, our joys and sorrows are one with Sudanese and Central American refugees, Gazan and Israeli children, the people of Ukraine, Polar Bears at risk on melting ice, mourning Elephant mothers, joyously sporting Right Whales, and grand-children racing down the soccer field. The interdependence of life connects us with those whom we will never meet: our grandchil-dren's grandchildren and the descendants of endangered species. The interdependence of life also inspires a mysticism of gratitude and love. There is, as I noted earlier, no "other." The mystical journey involves enlarging our circle of concern and compassion to embrace the whole earth and incarnate the spirit of Jesus and the Buddhist bodhisattva who sacrifice their immediate comfort to bring healing to all living creatures.

Christogenesis in Us. Jesus the Christ once stated "I am the light of the world." (John 8:12) He also reminded his followers that "You are the light of the world." (Matthew 5:14-16) The metaphysical author of John's Gospel expanded Jesus' claim to assert that "the true light that enlightens everyone was coming into the world." (John 1:9) We share in Christ's incarnational presence in the world. Christ is living within us and being born within us. Holding all things together and inspiring the evolution-ary process, Christ the Evolver is our deepest reality. Teilhard's mysticism sees Christ in our personal evolution and contribution to the evolutionary process and as the polestar aiming us toward God's Omega point. Christ is born in us and we midwife Christ's birth in creation.

Mysticism joins past, present, and future, the Christ that was, the Christ that is now inspiring us, and the Christ who lures us forward. Teilhard's mysticism integrates gratitude and appreciation of tradition; insight and inspiration in the evolving now; and eschatological anticipation of God's coming Omega point. Our faith is always in process as we midwife the evolutionary process and Christ's genesis in our own lives. Our mysticism, from a Teilhardian perspective, joins memory and appreciation, immediacy and wonder, and hope and anticipation. We are, as eschatological beings, living in an evolving now. We can live in confidence in God's vision for the future, knowing that "the power at work within us is able to accomplish abundantly far more than all we can ask or imagine, to him be glory in the church and in Christ Jesus to all generations, forever and ever. Amen" (Ephesians 3: 20-21).

CREATIVE MYSTICAL SYNTHESIS

Whitehead and Teilhard affirmed that God's revelation is universal and occurs within every existing thing. God is the ground and goal of our becoming self, the inspiration for each moment's self-creation. Matter is also alive with divinity and so is the child playing or the child reading with a grandparent or a monk at prayer. Inner fire energizes all things with a passion for the future. Deep down everyone is a potential mystic and can awaken to God's presence in the initial aim or the evolving Christ within.

The Divine Eros or Inner Fire enlightens each person and permeates all creation. No one is excluded from experiencing God, regardless of religion, culture, race, ethnicity, gender, sexual identity, or educational level. God is present in the secular as well as religious realms of life. Our mysticism leads to mission. Contemplation leads to action and claiming our role building the earth and promoting Christ's growth in the world.

While serious ecclesiastical and academic interfaith dialogue emerged following the deaths of Teilhard and Whitehead, their global cosmology and spirituality welcomes the insights of Buddhists, Hindus, First Americans, Jews, Muslims, Taoists, and other spiritual seekers. Whitehead believed that Buddhism and Christianity will flourish only through sharing each other's wisdom. In reflecting on the current spiritual situation, Whitehead observed, "instead of looking to each other for deeper meanings, have remained self-satisfied and unfertilized."[22] Both Buddhism and Christianity have suffered from their inflexibility in relationship to the rise of science.

Teilhard's writings are filled with allusions to other religious traditions. Teilhard distinguished between the "road of the East" and the "road of the West." While not completely restricted to Buddhism and Hinduism and not descriptive of all forms of Hindu and Buddhist spirituality, the "road of the East" leads to the quest for union with God, grounded in transcending the world of the flesh. Transcending all religious traditions, but related to a self-transcending Christianity, the "road of the West," which may include the insights of other religious traditions, unites union and differentiation. One in Christ, we retain our personality. Christ's personalization of the universe enables us to be fully ourselves, fully connected with the world embodied in human and non-human relationships, and fully connected with Christ. "To live the cosmic life is to live dominated by the consciousness that one is an atom in the body of the mystical and cosmic Christ. The man who so lives dismisses as irrelevant a host of preoccupations that absorb the interest of other men: his life is projected further, and his heart more widely receptive. There you have my intellectual testament."[23] As the evolutionary process converges in the Cosmic Christ becoming "all in all," each religion will realize its spiritual fullness. As they become more fully developed, inspired by the Christ-Omega, the world's religions will become partners in supporting the spirituality of their adherents and joining together as God's companions in healing the Earth. While Teilhard's vision was Christ-centered, and sometimes appears to diminish the gifts of other faiths, it was not exclusive. Christ, as Teilhard noted in one of his letters, is complemented and expanded by the dancing creativity of the Hindu God Shiva. In the end, as religions con-

---

22 Whitehead, *Religion in the Making*, 141.
23 Teilhard, *Writings in Times of War* (London: Collins, 1968), 70.

verge in partnership, they also rise in spirituality and realize the fullness of their vision in the Creative Union and Complexity of the Divine Omega.

In contrast to world denying spiritualities, Teilhard and Whitehead champion an embodied spirituality attentive to the earth and its seasons. Both would have been comfortable with a "new Francis," whose holistic approach to joining science and religion would re-enchant the world and recognize that even non-humans have spiritual lives.

For both Whitehead and Teilhard each moment can be a theophany revealing the divine. Burning bushes are everywhere and every dream can reveal a ladder of angels. The rock of ages reveals an inner fire. Teilhard's and Whitehead's this-worldly spirituality turns us toward, rather than away, from the world in the quest for God. Francis of Assisi's recognition that all things can praise their Creator is congruent with a Whiteheadian-Teilhardian spiritual orientation and is an inspiration, as we will see in the next chapter, to an emerging ecological consciousness. Perhaps the "new Francis" will be collective not individual. Perhaps, "we are the ones that we have been waiting for," as June Jordan challenges in her "Poem for the South African Women." Perhaps, God needs us to embody and push forward the evolutionary arc of history toward the Not-yet Omega!

Spiritual Practices: Incarnational Mysticism

The process theologies of Whitehead and Teilhard are profoundly incarnational. God is right here in this place. In Jacob's dream of a ladder of angels, the angels ascend from earth to heaven, and then return to earth with a heavenly vision. There are Earth angels and spirits everywhere among the Celts and indigenous people and the re-enchanted universe of Whitehead and Teilhard looks for the sacred in all things. There are "thin places" and "burning bushes" around every corner for those whose senses are awakened. Out of the that awakening comes wonder, gratitude, and the call to become God's companion in healing the world.

I believe that an evolutionary mysticism, congruent with a Whiteheadian-Teilhardian world view, involves five dynamically interdependent elements that can be integrated in our spiritual practices:

- *Awakening.* Divine revelation is universal in nature. Mysticism awakens us to God in this place and this place is wherever we are. We can experience God in the mundane and mystical. Paul's promise, "nothing can separate us from the love of God" is both a statement of divine protection and comfort and an affirmation that God is with us and can be experienced each moment of the day.

   We awaken to the holy in a variety of ways. A simple spiritual exercise involves feeling the pulse of the energy of love moving in and through you. Sitting in a comfortable position, building on the spiritual exercise from Chapter One, slowly focus on your breath, feeling the simple wonder of breathing. Let your breath connect you with the world around you. In the silence, affirm that you are a child of the universe, sustained by the universe. Feel the energy of love, symbolized by a golden light, filling you, healing you, and empowering you. The light of the world flows in and through you. You are the light of the world, and you can let God's light shine through you. God's light connects you with everything, energizing, enlightening, and evolving. Awaken to God's light and spread God's light everywhere.

- *Affirming.* The theologies of Whitehead and Teilhard affirm the good Earth and look for God's presence in history and embodiment. Our spiritual adventures join heaven and earth and seek to embody God's realm on earth as it is in heaven. The apostle Paul invites us to "be transformed by the renewing of your minds." (Romans 12:2)

One of the most effective ways to transform your mind is through the use of spiritual affirmations, or short sentences that describe the deeper realities of life and your nature as God's beloved child. Affirmations are a lens through which we view the world. Beginning with conscious repetition, they descend to the unconscious and become factors in renewing our vision of ourselves and the world.

The following affirmations are based on the metaphysical visions of Whitehead and Teilhard:

God inspires me with every breath.

The moral and spiritual arcs of the universe inspire and energize me.

God is constantly providing me with possibilities for spiritual transformation.

God's inner fire energizes, enlivens, and enlightens me.

My life is my gift to God.

I am God's companion in healing and evolving the Earth.

Repeat one or more of these affirmations, or an affirmation of your choice, several times daily to be a catalyst for spiritual transformation. You may choose to repeat one of these when you feel your spirit contracting from anxiety or alienation to liberate the Cosmic Christ within you.

• *Simplifying.* Revelation present in God's initial aim and in the "within" of our experience touches each moment of our lives. Still, we bring God's revelation to the surface of our consciousness by spiritual practices. (John 15:1-8) A process asceticism, grounded in the insights of Whitehead and Teilhard, involves focus rather than bodily denial. We can love God in the world of the flesh, as T.S. Eliot says, by aspiring to do "only one thing" – opening to God's inner and ambient presence - wherever we are. With Jesus, we trim all the branches that stand in the way of our relationship with God. In trimming or decluttering our lives, we more fully let God's light shine in our lives. Without abandoning the earth, we let go of everything that is superfluous or detracts from our spiritual growth and the wellbeing of those around us, including the planet.

In Charles Sheldon's classic on social gospel *In His Steps,* those who seek to follow Jesus' way are counseled to constantly ask, "What would Jesus do?" whenever they have an important decision. While this is good advice, the evolutionary spirituality of Whitehead and Teilhard adds additional counsels: "What adds to the beauty to this situation?", "How can I promote spiritual and planetary evolution in my decision-making?" We can, as Mother (Saint) Teresa asserts, "do something beautiful for God" wherever we are. Living with this focus awakens us to the energies of evolution and the moral arc of the universe. Moment by moment by acts of love and creativity, we build the framework for Christogenesis with God the Omega as our companion.

• *Expanding.* Whitehead describes religious adventure as a journey from self-interest to world loyalty. Teilhard speaks of the interplay of creative union and personal and relational differentiation. Peace and compassion come from expanding our sense of self beyond our experience to embrace the experiences of friends and strangers, humans and non-humans. This is what it means to have the "mind of Christ" or be a "Bodhisattva," who defers enlightenment until everyone is enlightened.

One path to an expanded consciousness is to see your connection with all things and realize that there is no "other." Take a moment to read Thomas Merton's account of unity with the passersby on Fourth and Walnut in Louisville, previously cited in this chapter. In your imagination, begin to visualize those persons with whom you are connected. Experience your unity. Now expand this vision to a neighbor...a stranger at the supermarket...a politician you support...a politician who offends you...feel your connection with the non-human world...with the planet...and beyond. You are connected to all things. There is no other. Conclude by praying that all creation finds wholeness in alignment with God's vision.

- *Transforming.* Our encounter with God inspires us to change the world. In speaking of the relationship of mysticism and social change, theologian-pastor-mystic Howard Thurman asserts that the mystic challenges everything that prevents persons from experiencing equality and justice. Our calling is to be agents of evolution and to support the moral and spiritual arcs of the universe – the emergence of Christ in the evolutionary process – by bringing forth the holiness and wholeness in every situation and claiming our vocation as God's companions in birthing Christ in our daily lives and the world.

Breathing with God's Creative Wisdom. While the first Genesis creation story (Genesis 1:1-2:4) has often been used to undergird unimaginative fundamentalist versions of "intelligent design," including "young earth" science and theology and descriptions of the creation of the universe occurring in six twenty-four-hour days, the poetic vision of Genesis, in contrast, describes an evolutionary unfolding of the universe and our planet. In this spiritual exercise, composed in the spirit of the imaginative approach to scripture championed by Ignatius of Loyola, the parent of the

Jesuit, or Society of Jesus, movement, let your mind roam free and
untrammeled.

In his own use of Ignatian "application of the senses," Teilhard would have appreciated an imaginative spiritual approach to
the evolutionary process.

Visualize yourself as an observer – or companion – of God in
the emergence of our universe. You may choose to follow these
steps:

- Begin with silence, opening to God's creative wisdom flowing
  through your imagination.

- Take time to read Genesis 1:1-2:4 slowly, opening to the wisdom beneath – and beyond – the words. Do not worry about
  any scientific inaccuracies, especially those surrounding "Day
  Four": this is an ancient pre-scientific text intended to inspire
  awe, wonder, and stewardship not a scientific treatise to
  explain the order of cosmic and planetary evolution. Experience God's delight at the formation of galaxies, our Milky
  Way, and our solar system.

- In the silence, visualize yourself in the first moments of creation, feel the winds of God's Spirit moving over the Deep,
  coaxing chaos toward order.

- Hear God's voice proclaim, "let there be light," and experience the dawn of the universe…and the birth of our sun and
  the lights of the sky.

- Experience the Divine Creator lovingly and gently, patiently
  and persistently, coaxing forth sky… land and sea…experi-
  ence the slow emergence of plants…and beyond.

- Feel God's joy as God beholds the beauty of creation, "it was
  good."

- Observe the emergence of simple and then more complex sea,
  land, and air creatures, and then share in God's pleasure in
  the emerging creaturely world.

- Observe the slow emergence of humankind, imaging God's creativity, and diverse in culture, race, and sexuality. Share in God's joy at the emergence of humankind and humankind's growing vocation to care for the earth and its creatures.

- Give thanks for the created world in all its wonder.

- Conclude by "resting" with God on the Sabbath, marveling at the wonder of the evolving universe and our place in it.

- Commit yourself to become a caretaker and gardener of creation, companioning God as you claim your vocation in "building the earth."

6

TRANSFORMING THE EARTH

Religion is world loyalty...God is that function in the world by reason of which our purposes are directed to ends which in our own consciousness are impartial to our own interests...of which our purposes extend beyond values to ourselves to values to others.[1]

In each soul, God loves and partly saves the whole world which that soul sums up in an incommunicable and particular way...By his fidelity [each one] must build -starting with the most natural territory of his own self – a work, an opus, into which something enters from all the elements of the earth. He makes his own soul throughout all his earthly days; and at the same time he collaborates in another work, in another opus, which infinitely transcends, while at the same time it narrowly determines, the perspectives of his individual achievement: the completing of the world.[2]

One of the most important questions life presents to us is "what is your vocation?" Or "what is your life's mission?" Our own destiny and the fate of the earth depend on how we and the communities and institutions of which we are a part answer the question of mission and vocation. Do we settle for the earth-destroying promises of the prosperity gospel, Chistian nationalism, unbridled capitalism, or soul-stifling communism? Or do we look for something more, a life that nourishes our souls and promotes the well-being of others? Does our vision of God ask too little of

---

1   Alfred North Whitehead, *Religion in the Making*, 59, 151-152.
2   Teilhard, *The Divine Milieu*, 60-61.

us in its baptism of the status quo? Or do we launch out in adventurous waters expecting great things from God and great things from ourselves, even when this involves conflict and sacrifice to ensure the flourishing of future generations? From a biblical perspective, these questions apply to nations and institutions as well as individuals.

My reflections on the nature of mission in Whitehead and Teilhard will be evocative and imaginative. Neither Whitehead nor Teilhard focused on the intricacies of personal and social ethics. Further, many of the issues that are central to today's ethical and political mission – such as ecology and climate change, civil rights, gender equality, and LGBTQ+ rights – had not yet taken center stage. Yet, their vision of an evolving, experiential, and empathetic universe in which God and humankind are companions in the moral and spiritual ascent of the human adventure has profound implications for our mission as persons of faith and planetary citizens in the twenty-first century.

Teilhard sees our calling as building the earth and preparing the way for the Cosmic Christ, the Omega Point toward which all creation leans. The coming of the Pleroma, the fullness of Christ, is fraught with challenges as I have noted throughout this book. The physical and institutional forces of entropy and division confront persons and nations every step of the way. The path of Christogenesis, the divinizing of matter and humankind and the healing and transforming of the earth, is our goal. Still, just as people ignored the message of the Hebraic prophets and conspired to crucify Jesus, many contemporary people and their political leaders turn away from God's vision of planetary wholeness, fanning the flames of division, incivility, alienation, nationalism, authoritarianism, and environmental destruction. Sadly, many of the evils in our time come from our Christian kin who place profit, nation, race, and power ahead of creative unity and planetary healing. Despite the counterforces to God's evolutionary mission, we must have faith that God will be "all in all" and that the forces of division and obstruction cannot in the long haul defeat the moral and spiritual arc of history.

Congruent with Teilhard, Whitehead saw the aim of the universe as the production of beauty. The philosopher saw history in terms of an adventure of ideas in which over centuries great ideas came to characterize the lives of individuals and nations. The experience of peace among individuals and nations involves moving from self-interest to world loyalty, and to identifying our self-interest with wider and wider circles of ethical concern. The quest for the great society and healthy planet, the great work of our time, involves the challenging of accepted values and our political and economic status quo in light of God's vision of truth, beauty, and goodness.

Martin Luther King relates an encounter in which metaphysics and mysticism joined hands to undergird prophetic mission. One evening in the early days of the Montgomery Bus Boycott, Martin Luther King received a phone call, threatening him and his family. Unable to sleep, King went downstairs to fix a pot of coffee. He was afraid for himself and his family and wanted to retreat from his vocation as a crusader for justice. In the midst of his spiritual crisis, King experiences an unexpected theophany, or encounter with God, that gives him courage for the long road to freedom.

> I was ready to give up. I tried to think of a way to move out of the picture without appearing to be a coward. In this state of exhaustion, when my courage was almost gone, I determined to take my problem to God. My head in my hands, I bowed over the kitchen table and prayed aloud.... "I am here taking a stand for what I believe is right. But now I am afraid. The people are looking to me for leadership, and if I stand before them without strength or courage, they too will falter. I am at the end of my powers. I have nothing left. I've come to the point where I can't face it alone."

In that rock-bottom moment, King discovered to his amazement he was standing on solid ground of God's presence and that nothing could separate him from the love God.

> At that moment I experienced the presence of the divine as I had never experienced him.
>
> It seems as though I could hear the quiet assurance of an inner voice, saying, "Stand up for righteousness, stand up for truth, God will be at your side forever.[3]

In the midst of his personal storm, Martin Luther King, like the Hebraic spiritual leader Elijah, hiding in a cave, experienced God's still small voice (1 Kings 19:11-13). King affirms, "the outer situation remained the same, but God had given me inner calm."[4] Three days later, King's home was bombed. Still, King remained rooted in God's faithfulness and the ultimate victory of the arc of justice in American history. King's encounter with God gave him strength and faith to face whatever storms would lie ahead not only in the Montgomery Bus Boycott but over the next decade as called America to seek justice and peace at home and abroad. King experienced God's protective presence and God's intimate relatedness. God is as near as our next breath, and with each breath comes the inspiration to creatively transform or, as Teilhard counseled, build the world.

Almost seven hundred and fifty years earlier, Francis of Assisi went to the Chapel of San Damiano seeking spiritual guidance. As he gazed at the cross, Francis heard the words, "Repair my church." At first, young Francis thought the revelation applied to the dilapidated chapel. After repairing three chapels, Francis realized that God was calling him to repair the spirit of Western Christianity and challenge the values of wealth, conquest, and power that characterized twelfth century religious life. Perhaps

---

3   Martin Luther King, Jr. *Testament of Hope: The Essential Writings and Speeches of Martin Luther King, Jr.* (edited by James M. Washington), (New York: HarperSanFrancisco, 1986), 509.

4   Ibid., 509.

God is calling us and our communities to be the "new Francis" in our contemporary commitments to heal the Earth through transformed lifestyles and corporate and political involvement.

Today, persons of faith are called to revive in novel ways the spiritual and ethical journeys of King and Francis. We need to repair the church. We need to liberate the church from static doctrine, backward looking theology, binary division of faith and science, and contemplation and action, and its complicity with racism, misogyny, homophobia, and nationalism. We also need to liberate the church and the community it serves to fulfill their vocation to heal and build the world. The church we seek to repair and embolden reflects the world in its wondrous diversity, not just a building or ecclesiastical institution, and we must share in furthering God's vision of creative union and unitive pluralism. Indeed, we should see the world as a sanctuary lit by the contrasting and complementary lights of the world's diverse religious and cultural traditions. A new vision of the world requires a new theology and spirituality, inspired by the God of Tomorrow and not the ruins of yesterday's institutional faith structures.

Our reflections on mission are not abstract, nor are they unrelated to our mysticism and metaphysical world views. We are on the "eve of destruction," to quote Barry McGuire's protest song of the sixties. Human and non-human life is being jeopardized by global climate change. Nations persist in stockpiling and threatening to use nuclear weaponry, despite the reality of "mutually assured destruction." The proliferation of conspiracy theories, fake news, incivility, violence, and racism threaten to undermine the structures of democracy, strides forward toward equality, and the very soul of the nation. Authoritarian religion and its worship of doctrine, exclusionary theology, and binary images of saved and unsaved and friend and enemy inspires authoritarian politics and anthropocentric economics. There seems to be a close connection between those who yearn for yesterday's God and the idyllic past and authoritarian and earth-destroying religious and political perspectives. The God of yesterday may have suited our ancestors but it pushes us toward the eve of disaster today.

We have ushered in the Anthropocene age of human technological power by which humankind can heal or destroy the planet. Over the past fifty years, we have gone from wall phones to cell phones, typewriters to computers, and paper calculations to artificial intelligence. The evolution of technology and communication is breathtaking in its incarnation of Teilhard's vision of the noosphere, the circle of consciousness surrounding the earth. The world has become a neighborhood, as Martin Luther King notes, and now it needs to become a "brotherhood," a place of kinship and common loving spirit. In "just such a time as this," our vocation is world transformation and healing whether this involves climate change, immigration, or the ethical and evolutionary use of Artificial Intelligence.

Religion is not necessarily good, Whitehead notes. Religious traditions inspire sacrifice for the greater good and nobility of spirit. They also inspire exclusivism, persecution, and crusade. The religion of the future must embrace love and not fear, and world loyalty rather than the idols of race, power, and nationalism. The religion of the future, inspired by the God of Tomorrow, must be forward-looking and science affirming. It must also inspire the affirmation of diversity and the quest for equality.

The interplay of life-affirming and open-spirited metaphysics, mysticism, and mission can lead us forward toward justice and equality, earth care, and ultimately the realization of God's realm on earth as it is in heaven. Guided by the insights of Whitehead and Teilhard, we can claim our vocation as God's partners in the next stages of evolution and world healing, the emergence of the Christ-consciousness and Christogenesis, in our world.

WHITEHEAD AND THE CALL TO WORLD LOYALTY

Whitehead contends that "your character is developed according to your faith." While Whitehead claims that religions have their origins in mystical experiences, he also believes that the cultivation of values and ethics is at the heart of religious experience: "a religion, on its doctrinal side, can thus be defined as a system of general truths which have the character of transforming character when they are sincerely held and vividly apprehended." Moreover, "in the long run your character of life depends upon your intimate convictions."[5] Despite the significance of religious belief in the positive formation of persons and institutions, religious doctrines are ambiguous. They can heal or harm, unite or destroy, persons and nations. According to Whitehead,

> religion is the last refuge of human savagery. The uncritical association of religion with goodness is directly negatived by the plain facts. Religion can be, and has been, the main instrument for progress. But if we survey the whole race, we must pronounce that generally it has not been so: "Many are called, but few are chosen."[6]

Healthy religion, in contrast, seeks to unite and affirm the wondrous diversity of human experience and honor the beauty of the Earth. The aim of religion, Whitehead believes, is the promotion of a world-consciousness, involving the movement from self-interest to world loyalty.[7] Life-supporting spirituality aligns itself with the "essential rightness of things" in which our faithfulness is inspired by love and not fear, gratitude and not obedience. In the evolution of religious experience, persons initially "study the will of God that he will preserve you." Higher, rational religions, "study his goodness in order to be like him. It is the difference between the enemy you conciliate and the companion whom you imitate."[8] Healthy spirituality promotes divinization, the imitation and incarnation of God's Spirit in everyday life and political and economic decision-making. Further, the process of divinization, embodying God's character in our behaviors, chal-

---

5 Whitehead, *Religion in the Making*, 15.
6 Ibid., 36.
7 Ibid., 39.
8 Ibid., 40.

lenges us to love the world that God loves as we align ourselves with the spiritual and moral arcs of history.

Whitehead asserts that "there is but one religious dogma in debate: What do you mean by 'God'?" All other theological questions flow from understanding of the Ultimate Reality and its relationship to creation, humankind, and history. In that spirit, biblical scholar Terry Fretheim claims that the nature of the God in whom you believe is more important than whether or not you believe in God. Our visions of God shape our values, behavior, politics, and sense of mission.

Process theologian Bernard Loomer contrasts two images of God: relational and unilateral. Unilateral images of God privilege authority and power. God calls but doesn't listen. God acts but doesn't respond. God coerces but does not cooperate. God shapes but is not affected by the world. Communication is one-way. God is the ultimate authority, silencing all other voices except God's appointed emissaries. Creaturely creativity and innovation are affront to God's power and lead to dire consequences for humankind.[9] For those who step out of line and oppose the status quo and its authoritarian God and the patriarch's followers, the cost is retribution, and divine retribution meted out in this lifetime by those who perceive themselves (falsely) as God's emissaries, who proudly announce to their adoring followers, "I am your retribution."

In contrast to images of divine power as unilateral and authoritarian, Whitehead and his student Bernard Loomer view God's power as relational and loving. God's love is responsive as well as creative. God is the ultimate recipient of the world's joy and sorrow, the fellow sufferer who understands and the joyful companion who celebrates. God rules – or guides – by love, not fear.

Whitehead's God delights in loving and supportive relationships. In contrast to unilateral and authoritarian visons of God, which see love in terms of obedience and control, Whitehead

---

9   Bernard Loomer, "Two Conceptions of Power." *Process Studies* 6:1, 5-32.

affirms that God's quest for beauty inspires innovation and creativity. God rejoices in responsible freedom and creativity. Divine relationality inspires a democracy of revelation in which there are no outsiders and all people have voice and value. God delights in creativity and surprise and sees our creativity as opening the door to greater expressions of God's own creativity. In contrast to the God of relationship and creativity, authoritarian visions of God are binary and divide the world into saved and unsaved, chosen and rejected, and friend and foe. From the perspective of authoritarian religion, foes and those rejected by God such as indigenous peoples and slaves, have neither value nor deserve our ethical consideration. To the dismay of the followers of yesterday's authoritarian God, the relational universality of Whitehead's and Teilhard's God leads to honoring diversity in flora and fauna, bird, fish, insect, and mammal, and delight in the wondrous diversity of the human species. God and humanity are constantly motivated by the questions, "How can we support? How can we protect?" and "What can we learn?" from the holy otherness of humankind and the non-human world.

The relational God inspires followers whose mission is to add to the creativity, beauty, and diversity of the world. To add beauty to the world has practical consequences in political as well as personal life: we must commit as persons and nations to ensure the basics of institutional and environmental health, diet, education, housing, self-determination, and human rights. From a relational perspective, economically wealthy nations must look beyond their self-interest and be willing to sacrifice to advance these basics among nations whose citizens are struggling for survival and security.

A relational God encourages positive and affirmative relationships that include outsiders as well as allies and this means that we see both documented and undocumented immigrants as God's children as we address the inequalities and violence that lead to migration. Our mission is the promotion of beauty, complexity, and evolution in our citizenship and intimate relationships.

Mission in an Interdependent Universe. Empathy and relationship are central to Whitehead's vision of reality. All creatures are connected to their immediate environment and the wider world. There are no absolute and impregnable borders when it comes to the human and non-human, despite our need to privilege some relationships and loyalties over others. While I love my country and respect its laws, borders, and unique identity, following Teilhard and Whitehead's planetary vision, I cannot morally privilege US citizens over immigrants or persons in other countries. God's love is global, embracing humankind in all its ethnic, racial, cultural, religious, and sexual diversity. What happens in China, Israel, Gaza, Guatemala, Ethiopia, or Ukraine shapes the quality of life in the United States and implicitly my own quality of experience. The well-being of undocumented persons shapes the wellbeing of legal citizens. Their pain and the injustices they experience – not to mention the incivility and hate perpetrated by isolationist politicians – undermines the quality of each American's experience. Embracing and supporting LGBTQ+ persons heals their wounds and the woundedness of heterosexuals. We cannot exist and flourish as a nation and people without affirming the holy otherness of diverse nations and people.

No one captures the mission of relatedness more inspirationally than Martin Luther King, whose theological vision was influenced by process-relational theology. Reflecting the spirit of the relational God, King's words, like Psalm 148, bear repeating as witness to the world Teilhard and Whitehead envision:

> It all boils down to this, that all life is interrelated. We are caught in an inescapable network of mutuality, tied into a single garment of destiny. Whatever affects one directly, affects all indirectly. We are made to live together because of the interrelated structure of reality.[10]
>
> For some strange reason I cannot be what I ought to be until you are what you ought to be. And you can

---

10 Martin Luther King, *Testament of Hope* (New York: Harper One), 254.

never be what you ought to be until I am what I ought
to be."[11]

In the metaphysics and mysticism of interconnectedness,
our mission is grounded in our feelings of empathy for every created life. There is no "other." There is no "stranger" or "foreigner."
Metaphysics and mysticism lead to practice: our mission is to contribute to God's aim of beauty by compassionate relationships and
the creation of empathetic and just institutional, economic, and
governmental structures. Despite the limits implicit in the USA's
two-party political system, political leaders and citizens alike must
look beyond the wellbeing of their constituents, supporters, political policies, and national priorities to work toward justice, hos-
pitality, and healing beginning with our nation and expanding to
the whole Earth. To be faithful to God, we must privilege compassion and community and deemphasize party spirit, incivility,
and alienation in political policy. We must join competition with
cooperation and compassion to secure the future of the Earth and
its peoples.

Morality applies to the relationships of nations as well as individuals. Our political mission is to create programs that foster
economic well-being, human rights, and Earth care in our land
and beyond our borders. Our goal should be cooperative relationships that benefit each nation's peoples in terms of an updated ecological and Earth-affirming vision of Franklin Delano Roosevelt's
"four freedoms" – freedom of speech, of religion, from want, and
from fear.

Honoring Experience in All its Diversity. Whitehead asserts
that to exist is to be a center of experience. While complexity and
intensity of experience varies among species and flora and fauna,
to experience is to be a locus of value and holiness and value is
universal. Whitehead challenges us to expand our ethical mission
to include the non-human as well as human world. Non-humans
feel joy and pain and have a desire, at least in some "primitive"

---

11 *A Knock at Midnight* (New York: Warner Books, 2000), 208.

manner, not only live, but live well and better. American poet
Robert Frost describes "a considerable speck," a mite running
across the paper on which he intends to pen a few lines of poetry.
At first glance, he is tempted to kill the mite with a tap of his
pen, letting the ink be the mite's quietus. Then, he looks closer
at the barely visible creature and realizes that it has purposes of its
own. It doesn't want to die. It scurries across the paper and then
pauses as if to accept its fate. Frost desists and spares its life. Frost
concludes his poem with words with which many a teacher can
identify.

> I have a mind myself and recognize
>   Mind when I meet it in any guise
>   No one can know how glad I am to find
>   On any sheet the least display of mind.[12]

Ethicists have noted that devaluing the non-human world is
often connected with devaluing our human kin, most especially
those who are our "enemies" or "differ" from us. If one part of the
world is seen as valueless, we can extend this denigration to other
parts of our world, including other human communities. Rele-
gation of indigenous people, women, members of the LGBTQ+
community, and persons of color to second class and often sub-
human ethical and legal status testifies to indivisibility of value
and ethical consideration. We live in a God-filled and value-filled
world, inspiring us to protect and support others' experiences,
value and fulfillment. Repairing the world involves confession
and sacrifice and the willingness to enact wise reparations to promote equal starting points for those whose ancestors experienced
slavery, genocide, and social marginalization. It means that our
mission, within the context of the common good, is to let a thousand flowers bloom, a multitude of voices speak, and diverse opinions go forth.

Promoting Value. We live in a God-filled universe. The heavens shout God's glory. The endangered Right Whale breaching

12 Robert Frost, "A Considerable Speck."

praises its Creator. Pangolins and primates yearn for abundant life. Sloth mothers nurture their clinging babies, and trees and insects dance in the give and take of pollination and sustenance. The whole earth reflects the quest for beauty. The competition and collaboration of evolution aims toward complexity and intensity of experience. A God-filled universe is also a value filled universe in which, as Whitehead asserts, every creature aims at value for itself and for its immediate environment. Morality is grounded in the sense of worth, inherent in every existing thing. Accordingly, we have no right to intentionally debase the value of things, whether human or non-human.[13]

In a world of competing ethical goods, whether in economics, human rights and responsibilities, reproductive justice and fetal life, our mission is to promote the value of individuals and communities. While we must weigh and balance situationally the apparent and sometimes conflicting values of fetuses and women, citizens and non-citizens, human dietary needs and farm animals, God's aim at beauty requires us to consider the wellbeing of each creature both for itself and the world around it. "Reverence for life" is at the heart of the spiritual journey, ethical behavior, and institutional and political values. While the concept of "reverence for life" is more often known through its absence than affirmation in human decision-making, nevertheless, our recognition of the ubiquity of value requires compassion, gratitude, and a strong justification for behaviors that harm our fellow creatures. The universality of value compels us to minimize suffering and maximize enjoyment and prevent in advance situations in which mass suffering is a possibility.

In a world without clear borders, national security must be weighed with planetary wellbeing. Economic growth must include the wellbeing of workers, especially in developing nations. Gratitude and wonder, radical amazement and the quest for beauty of experience must guide our personal and corporate missions. Inherent in Whitehead's thought is an ecological consciousness,

13 Whitehead, *Modes of Thought,* 109-111.

which challenges us to live simply individually while we advocate for institutional and corporate reduction of fossil fuel usage, aim at net zero emissions, and protect non-human life as well as forests, grasslands, and bodies of water. The universality of value challenges us to live more simply so others, including our non-human companions, may simply live (Elizabeth Ann Seton), and to sacrifice short term values for survival and quality of life of our human and non-human companions.

Partnership in an Open Universe. Open and relational theologian Thomas Oord asserts that "God can't" change the course of a river or disease on God's own, or secure justice and peace without human cooperation.[14] Centuries before Oord and Whitehead articulated a vision of a God who needs our efforts to achieve God's vision, the Spanish mystic Teresa of Avila (1515-1582) professed:

> Christ has no body but yours,
> No hands, no feet on earth but yours,
> Yours are the eyes with which he looks
> Compassion on this world,
> Yours are the feet with which he walks to do good,
> Yours are the hands, with which he blesses all the world.
> Yours are the hands, yours are the feet,
> Yours are the eyes, you are his body.
> Christ has no body now but yours,
> No hands, no feet on earth but yours,
> Yours are the eyes with which he looks
> compassion on this world.
> Christ has no body now on earth but yours.

A Whiteheadian mantra is that the world lives by the incarnation of God. In an incarnational universe, we are God's embodiments and agents in the adventure of healing the Earth. The universe is incomplete and a better future is open for God and us. Divine power neither predestines nor coerces. Each moment

14 Thomas Jay Oord, *God Can't.* (Nampa, ID: Sacra Sage Press, 2019).

of experience emerges from many causes, one of which is God. God and our own creative freedom shape the world in which we live and the institutions that bring life and death to communities. Although God does not have a one pre-determined end or ideal future in Whitehead's vision of the God-world relationship, God's aim is toward Shalom, wholeness, and beauty, manifest in the world as it is and looking toward the world that could be. God's aims are promoted and sabotaged by our behaviors and commitments at the individual and corporate levels. Our mission is, as Jewish spirituality proclaims, *tikkun 'olam*, mending or healing the world. The world is saved one moment and act at a time, grounded in alignment of our lives with God's vision. "Earth is in the balance," as former USA Vice-President Al Gore asserts. We make a difference, healing or harming, and promoting or preventing God's highest ideals to come to emerge in our world.

Politics and business, like personal life, are ultimately spiritual issues in which our vision of God, power, and the future inspires creation or destruction. God will not save us or evolve humankind and the planet apart from our efforts. There is no Plan B for planet earth, divine rescue operation that will deliver us from self-destruction, or datable Second Coming of Jesus to save us from our folly. Not even our science will save us if we turn away from God's evolving vision of truth, beauty, and goodness for all creation. Healing the earth is our vocation in partnership with the Artist, Poet, and Lover of the Universe. Our mission, personally and corporately, is to be agents of Earth healing and Earth preservation.

TEILHARD AND OUR MISSION OF BUILDING THE EARTH

Teilhard was a theologian-scientist with a mission. The theory of evolution revealed a value-laden universe. The universe is the move, bringing forth greater unity and complexity. Cooperation as well as competition characterizes the ascent from single celled organisms to humankind. With the appearance of humankind, especially human language, culture, technology, and religion, humans have become partners in evolution. The non-human world is valuable and is energized by a fire within to reach higher in its evolutionary journey.[15] As the pinnacle of Earth life, humans can reach higher than they can imagine, building cities, creating civilizations, shaping the environment, and promoting justice as a matter of intentionality as well as instinct. The fire of the spirit burning within humankind calls us forward and upward and gives us the choice to align ourselves with Evolving Christ or stand in the way of God's future vision. We have a mission, collaborating "in another work, in another opus, which infinitely transcends, while at the same time it narrowly determines, the perspectives of his individual achievement: the completing of the world."[16] Although Teilhard emphasizes human responsibility and agency in forwarding the evolutionary process and realizing the Omega Point, he also recognizes with gratitude and affirmation the long evolutionary journey in the non-human world from which we came. Christocentrism promotes the geosphere and biosphere as well as the noosphere on the way to the fulfillment of the Christ-Omega, Christosphere.

Building the Earth and Healing the Planet. Individually and corporately humans share in the Great Mission of partnering with God in the evolutionary process. At times, Teilhard's words suggest that history is moving toward a predetermined fulfillment, a "manifest destiny," in which Christ becomes all and all, uniting creative union with complexity and individuality. Teilhard believes that despite our waywardness, we cannot defeat God's quest at spiritualizing the Earth. Empowered by the Christ-Omega, the divinization of humankind and the earth is connected with human efforts. Giving birth to Christ is our vocation and Christ-Omega is our destiny. But, the hour and the day of fulfillment depends upon us as well as God. God needs our evolutionary actions to become fully God in our world.

---

15 Sheri Kling, "Toward the Fire Must Teilhard's View of Human Consciousness be Anti-Ecological?" Unpublished essay, 2011.

16 Teilhard, *The Divine Milieu*, 60-61.

In our current ambiguous world of unity and divisiveness, creativity and destructiveness, we have a clear mission – build the earth. Mirroring Christ's words to Francis, "repair my church," for it is in disarray and chaos, we hear within our spirits the message, "build the earth," stand with creation, confront injustice, speak for the voiceless, honor God's creatures everywhere. Earth building embraces the well-being of all creatures, not just humans. Although Teilhard centers his work on humankind's role in Christogenesis, in birthing Christ in our world, humanity is intricately connected with the totality of the universe journey.

We are the children of the Big Bang. We are star stuff and descendants of amoeba. We rise with and from our apelike ancestors. We are one with the evolutionary process from which we have come. For all that comes before us, we should be grateful. With Meister Eckhart, if the only prayer we make, as we consider the long and perilous journey of evolution, is "thank you" this will suffice as we recall those who came before us, both human and non-human, who sacrificed that we might be at this point in the evolutionary journey. We wouldn't be here at this critical moment of planetary history apart from the suffering and sacrifice, and the creativity and commitment of our human and non-human ancestors. We must, to use a phrase from the wisdom of the African religion – Yoruba spirituality – commit ourselves to practicing in this lifetime our role as being "good ancestors" to those who follow us. Their sacrifice inspires the commitments and sacrifices we make in our time to further the coming of the Cosmic Christ in our world.

In pondering the long evolutionary journey of which humankind is a part and now the creaturely creative center, Teilhard would have appreciated the words of his younger contemporary, Dag Hammarskjold (1905-1961), who served as General Secretary of the United Nations during Teilhard's residence in New York City.

> For all that has been – thanks!
> For all that shall be – yes![17]

---

17 Dag Hammarskjold, *Markings* (New York: Knopf, 1964), 89 .

Our mission, born of gratitude for God's presence as the energy of love igniting the evolutionary process and those creatures whose lives gave birth to our evolutionary journey, is grounded in the great "yes" of the future. Our mission to build the earth involves partnering with God in midwifing the Christosphere from its biospheric and noospheric ancestors.

From Teilhard's perspective, our mission is always concrete and historical because evolution is always concrete and historical. Evolution embraces rocks, cells, dinosaurs, Right Whales, chimpanzees, flourishing human children, and the impact of climate change on seas, forests, and weather patterns. As God's hands, hearts, heads, and feet, building the earth involves choosing to be agents of environmental justice, human rights, healthy technology, and global peacemaking. As evolution becomes conscious of itself, the contours of humanity's mission to build the earth come to us in the integration of the daily news and the challenges of prophets to "let justice roll down like waters and righteousness like an ever-flowing stream" (Amos 5:24). Although the task of giving birth to the Pleroma, Christ-consciousness, is daunting, we must seek to invite all creation to experience God's vision of an abundant, interdependent, and unified planet in which all creatures fulfill their destiny in God's as cells in the body of Christ.

Joining Unity and Otherness. Teilhard is the apostle of evolutionary unity. All creation is aimed at the Omega Point, the Fullness of Christ. Although we often are mired in rugged individualism and divisive independence, we are all connected as cells in the body of Christ. The universe strives toward conscious and creative union and complexity. Creative union, however, embraces diversity and pluralism. As a panentheistic theologian, recognizing that God is in the world, responsive to the world, and yet more than the world, Teilhard's theological bias is toward the integration of unity and diversity. Plurality is present even in the Triunity of God's existence. The Father, Son, and Holy Spirit, or Creator, Redeemer, and Sustainer, joins the one and the many, without disruption or monotony. The Trinity is the ultimate model as well as source of an interdependent, unified, and diverse creation. From Teilhard's perspective the health of the whole and the health of the parts depend on one another. Evolution works in individuals to move forward the human race and the planet, and the progress of the human race and the planet in the evolutionary process nurtures individual creativity.

Our mission is to promote union without uniformity and diversity without division. Too often the quest for unity issues in enforced uniformity in which the voices of religious, ethnic, gender, sexual, political, and racial minorities have been silenced or eliminated altogether. This affirmation of unity and diversity in the quest for national and planetary community involves balancing and moving forward the common good of communities as well as the value of individuals and minority voices in community. In the amazing diversity of life, human minorities and non-human voices are essential to the health of the whole. In the evolution of religion, the voices of heretics must be heard and not silenced. We need Augustine's sense of divine providence and human sin and Pelagius' vision of human possibility and the divine in every child. The old-time religion gains passion from welcoming the unfettered winds of the Spirit. Indeed, liberated from yesterday's doctrines, one of the verses of that childhood hymn says:

> Give me that old time religion,
>   Makes me love everybody,
>   Makes me love everybody,
>   Makes me love everybody,
>   It's good enough for me.

The dynamic connection of one and many applies to nations as well as communities. Teilhard notes that "the age of nations has passed." Going beyond national sovereignty seems a fantasy today. Nationalism is on the rise and promotes ruthlessness by white USA conservative Christians. National leaders threaten nuclear war and compete for resources. Politicians in the USA speak of states seceding from the union. Millions are food and shelter insecure while others live in comfort and luxury. We need to be pioneers of political and national self-transcendence. While we may not immediately be able to forge a planetary governmental unity, with each national community seeing itself as a cell in the life of the planet, willing to sacrifice for the survival and flourishing of other communities, we can challenge our political leaders to love the citizens of other lands with the same spirit as they love their own citizens. We can examine our contribution to global climate change, unjust economic conditions, famine, and political instability, and commit ourselves to creating structures of health, justice, security, and Earth care in partnership with other nations. We can ponder an international tithe in which wealthier nations provide lifesaving and development resources to impoverished nations without the pressures of political quid pro quos. In Teilhard's universe, not only is the glory of God a fully alive human, but God's radiance is embodied in a fully alive planet.

Supporting Christ. Classical and conservative Christian theology views God as all-powerful, fully able to achieve any of God's goals without human assistance. God is eternal and complete, needing nothing from us. What happens in the world, for good or ill, flows from God's omnipotent hand. Although we feel as if we are agents of our destiny, God is in control and everything from our births and deaths, the election of a president, a cancer diagnosis, and climate change is determined and enacted according to God's good pleasure. Guided by the vision of an omnipotent, binary God, we believe that the earth will be fulfilled or destroyed without either our consent or agency. We are, as the saying goes, "damned if we do, and damned if we don't." If God is in control and will eventually replace this earth with another as a prelude to our heavenly destination, there is no need to seek justice or address global climate change and species extinction. It is all in God's hands. And, if we trust the messages of the end-time preachers, we can drill, baby, drill, and consume with abandon, and without regard to the Earth, for our planet's days are numbered, and we might as well use up the planet while we're waiting for Jesus.

In contrast, Teilhard and Whitehead describe a relational God, who works within our world and our lives, inviting us to be responsible agents and companions in building the earth. In a way that astounds us, the God of the universe needs us! This world matters and is essential to God's vision of the future. Although Christ the Evolver will be "all in all," we play an essential role in the achievement of Christ's fullness on earth.

No one captures our vocation in times of crises and uncertainty more poignantly than Etty Hillesum (1914-1943), a young Jewish woman and a contemporary of both Teilhard and Whitehead, who died during the Holocaust. Pondering the contrast between the beauty of the earth and the horrific evil of Nazi genocide, Hillesum discovers that God needs her as much as she needs God. Her commitments play a role in tipping the world from ugliness to beauty and death to life, and she can choose fidelity in a world gone mad.

> I shall try to help you God, to stop my strength from ebbing away, though I cannot vouch for it in advance. But one thing is becoming increasingly clear to me: that You cannot help us, but we must help You help ourselves. And that is all that we can manage today and all that really matters: that we safeguard that little place of You, God, in ourselves. And, perhaps others as well. Alas, there doesn't seem to be much You Yourself can do about our circumstances, about our lives. You cannot help us, but we must help You and defend Your dwelling place in us to the last.[18]

Our task as God's companions in the most desperate situations for ourselves and the planet, Hillesum believes, is to "be willing to act as a balm for all wounds."[19]

The evolving Energy of Love, incarnate in Christ, moves forward despite human waywardness. God's arc of evolution and jus-

18 Etty Hillesum, *An Interrupted Life* (New York: Picador, 1966) 178.
19 Ibid., 231

tice cannot be defeated by our self-interest and short-sightedness. But, still God needs our help to advance God's vision "on earth as it is in heaven." We are the agents of unity amid diversity. We are the healers of the earth, God's emissaries to a broken planet. We are the balm for the wounded and the physicians of planetary recovery. God and the world, God and each of us, work together to bring healing to a "groaning creation." That is our vocation and fulfillment.

CREATIVE MISSIONAL SYNTHESIS

We have a mission, according to both Whitehead and Teilhard, and this mission involves healing the Earth, personally and corporately, in partnership with the Creative Wisdom aiming at beauty, complexity, and the marriage of unity and diversity. God needs us to bring God's vision of truth, beauty, and goodness to the Earth. God needs us to be prophets of world-loyalty in which nations, national leaders, and ourselves go beyond self-interest, greed, and power to join in healing the earth. In the world of Teilhard and Whitehead, everyone matters. Humans need the non-human world and the non-humans need us. Our agency within the noosphere and the age of the Anthropocene, the age of humanity's shaping of the planet, can foster flourishing and growth to the Earth, or bring famine, destruction, species extinction, and climate deterioration. While God's truth is marching on in the growth of civilization and the evolutionary process, our calling is to march along with God's vision and to embody Earth-healing by our actions. We have a responsibility to God and the evolutionary process whether the goal of evolution is assured or significantly dependent on our actions.

Whitehead and Teilhard may differ in their certainty in terms of the exact timing of the realization and nature of God's aim of history, in terms of whether there is one final goal or many possibilities, and in terms of whether God's vision must prevail or we can impede the embodiment of God's vision. Still, both claim that our efforts are essential in promoting the moral and spiritual arcs of history and evolution, whether they are open-ended or clearly demarcated. Even if God's Omega will be achieved on earth as it is in heaven, our mission is to be agents of the future in partnership with God, to repair and heal persons, nations, and the planet.

When he walked with Martin Luther King, Jewish theologian Abraham Joshua Heschel recalled that it felt like his legs were praying. We must, as the South African hymn proclaims, march in the light of God, *Siyahamba,* towards God's vision of Shalom, the Omega that calls us forward.

SPIRITUAL PRACTICES: BUILDING THE EARTH

Whitehead and Teilhard join the inner and outer and personal and planetary in their understanding of mission. While religion has to do with the self and cultural transcendence of individualism, and in the moral sphere, self-interest, what is hidden becomes public not only in its impact on the next moment of experience but in our values, commitments, choices, and citizenship. The spiritual, moral, and physical arcs of evolution flow through us. Whether we describe these arcs in terms of God's initial aim or the passion for evolution within us, these arcs aim at intense beauty and delight in the present moment and for the relevant and ultimately cosmic future. God intends to promote building the Earth by God's presence in our lives. As evolution becomes conscious of itself, we humans can lean toward these aims or arcs of evolution, building a beautiful earth and incarnating Christ's vision right where we are. We can live our lives as anticipations of the realization of the Christ-Omega Point or God's vision of Beauty.

Alignment with the Spiritual and Moral Arcs of Evolution. In this spiritual practice, we will begin with silence and then spiritual reflection. Jesus said "ask and it will be given, seek and you will find, and knock and the door will open." In seeking, asking, and knocking in quest of God's wisdom, we will receive the guidance we will need to move forward step by step, trusting that deep down our experience reveals God's initial aim, or possibility, or the contours of God's evolutionary passion. In this spirit, strive to become aware of God's spiritual, moral, and evolutionary arcs running through your life.

You may take time daily for quietly opening to divine wisdom. Simply listening for God's whispered word emerging in your experience. While not expecting complete or absolutely clear answers – although at times such answers come – look for inner yearnings, insights, or intuitions. When you receive these moments of guidance, pray for these to unfold in your life and relationships. Pray that your inner and outer behavior, the within and without, are congruent with God's evolutionary vision.

As a form of self-awareness, you may choose to take time for an "examen" or "examination of experience" each day in which after a time of silence and gratitude, you look back at your day, reflecting on times you were in alignment with God's evolutionary vision and times when you turned away from your call to companionship in building the earth. You may reflect on the question: When did you promote beauty and unity and planetary well-being and when did you focus on self-interest to the exclusion of the welfare of others? Conclude by asking for God's guidance and strength to become more fully aligned with God's evolutionary vision.

The Personal and Planetary Healing through Healing Touch. Whitehead and Teilhard agree with the wisdom of Jewish mysticism: when you save a soul, you save the world; when you destroy a soul, you destroy the world. Our personal and corporate mission is to be God's companions in *tikkun 'olam,* healing the world. While I affirm the wisdom of Jewish mysticism, I believe that the world is also saved one moment and action at a time. Accordingly, we can claim our vocation as God's moment-by-moment companions in bringing forth the inner fire of evolution to heal the world. We can mediate the energy of loving evolution to creation by acts of kindness, reconciliation, and reparation. We can also mediate the Divine Eros by healing touch, which joins the within and without, and personal well-being and spiritual growth, to heal persons and the planet.

Individual and global healing are united for Teilhard and Whitehead. I have been a Reiki Healing Touch practitioner since the mid-1980's and a Reiki Master/Teacher since the mid-1990's. Reiki, a form of healing energy transmitted either by laying on of hands or at a distance, has become central to my personal self-care and spiritual growth, my pastoral ministry, and relationships with friends. Similar to Chinese practices such as Tai Chi and Qigong, Reiki – or divine energy – mediates the *chi* or *ki*, to oneself or others, balancing the flow and intensity of energy in our lives to promote peace of mind, overall well-being, and on occasion surprising naturalistic healing. Grounded in the use of spiritual symbols, whose role is to open persons to the ever-present divine energy flowing in and through us and all things, Reiki is a simple way to enhance the moral and spiritual arcs of evolution flowing through our lives to bring healing energy to the world.

In the practice of Reiki, I begin a "treatment" with silence and then, typically, touch with a flat palm the various energy centers (chakras) of my own or another's body. Similar to the Christian liturgical practice of laying on of hands, the gentle still touch relaxes, comforts, and expands and balances the universal energy within us. Reiki joins the within and without, the physical and spiritual in harmony as a way of healing our lives in this moment of time. Like the practice of meditation, the practice of Reiki and other healing arts in community raises the healing energy of communities and enhances the process of evolution from noosphere to Christophere. In certain situations, I give non-local or distant reiki as a way of opening political leaders to the "better angels of their natures." In healing ourselves and others, we heal the Earth and become pioneers in planetary evolution.

Healing the Soul of the Nation and the Planet. After marching with Martin Luther King, Rabbi Abraham Joshua Heschel exclaimed, "I felt like my legs were praying." Healing the soul of our nation and planet, reflecting our vocation to build the earth, is the gift of prayer and meditation in which we align ourselves with the moral, spiritual, and evolutionary arcs of history. The journey inward, the journey within, inspires us to the journey outward, the journey without, in positive actions for social transformation. We are called, as Mother (Saint) Teresa of Calcutta counsels, "to do something beautiful for God" in our personal relationships, vocational life, and national and planetary citizenship.

The survival of our planet and nation is at risk. The noosphere, the envelope of interdependent consciousness surrounding the earth, needs healing and direction to realize its goal of becoming the Christ-Omega. God needs our prayers, but prayers are not enough. We need to act for nation and planet. We need to move from self-interest and nationalism to world loyalty.

Reflecting on the wisdom you have received in this text – and in the two previous exercises in this chapter: Where do you feel called to act to heal and build the world? In what ways can you further the moral and spiritual arcs of evolution as God's companion in building the earth. In the spirit of Isaiah's encounter with God in the Jerusalem Temple (Isaiah 6:1-8), God is pleading, "Whom shall we send and who will go for us?" What will it mean for you to say, "Here I am, send me" in the context of your personal responsibilities? What does it mean for a congregation, community, political leader, or nation to say "Here we are send us"? Pray for guidance in your conduct in both the micro world of home, work, and church and the macro world of citizenship, institutions, and governments. Even if the guidance you receive is incomplete, take the first steps in becoming a world-builder by your actions and commitments. Let your prayers and reflections be transformed into world-building actions.

7

AN UNFINISHED ADVENTURE

God is the ideal companion who transmutes what has been lost into a living fact within his own nature. He is the mirror which discloses to every creature its greatness…Every fact is what it is, a fact of pleasure, a fact of joy, a fact of suffering. In its union with God that fact is not a total loss, but on its finer side is an element to be woven immortally into the rhythm of mortal things. Its very evil becomes a stepping stone in the all-embracing ideals of God.[20]

Let us look at the earth around us. What is happening under our eyes among the mass of peoples? What is the cause of the disorder in society, the uneasy agitation, these swelling waves, these whirling and mingling currents, and these turbulent and formidable new impulses? Mankind is visibly passing through a crisis of growth. Mankind is becoming dimly aware of its shortcomings and its capacities…It sees the universe growing luminous like the horizon just before sunrise. It has a sense of premonition and expectation.[21]

We live in a luminous, God inspired universe. The Earth is growing and groaning. As we look toward the future, we find ourselves gazing at both the precipice of self-destruction and the horizon of hope. We too are groaning as we view the damage we have done to our planet. We are also glowing with anticipation of the world of creative union, complexity, and beauty that calls us

---

20 Whitehead, *Religion in the Making*, 149.
21 Teilhard, *The Divine Milieu* (New York: *Harper* and Row, 1960), 153.

forward, inspiring us to be midwives of the future and repairers of the rubble.

We are earthly stewards of evolution and our stewardship has brought out wonders of science and technology and also the possibility of using our technology and science to render our planet uninhabitable. We can live by love or fear. We can be guided by reason or the reptilian brain. We can be world loyal or self-interested. The growth of the noosphere can lead to a dead planet or be a thoroughfare to the divinization of the Earth and us. As the apostle Paul notes in Romans 8, one of the greatest documents in Christian history.

> For the creation waits with eager longing for the revealing of the children of God, for the creation was subjected to futility not of its own will but by the will of the one who subjected it in hope that the creation itself will be set free from its bondage to decay and will obtain the freedom of the glory of the children of God. We know that the whole creation has been groaning in labor pains until now; and not only the creation, but we ourselves, who have the first fruits of the Spirit, for we wait for our adoption, the redemption of our bodies. For in hope we were saved…For we hope for what we do not see, we wait for it with patience. (Romans 8:19-25)

Teilhard and Whitehead are apostles of hope amid discord and adventure as the counterforce to entropy. They are hopeful realists and realistic prophets. They heard the groans of creation in living through two world wars and witnessing the atomic bomb. They leaned forward with the adventures of civilization-transforming ideas, knowing that an unseen energy pushed forward the arc of spiritual, political, and biological evolution. They knew that the flourishing of humankind can come only through love that awakens our connection to one another and gives birth to a politics of loving evolution. We cannot be saved alone. We must be saved with all creation, and in our taking our responsibility as agents of evolution, we bring the created world to fulfillment.

We must align ourselves with the God of Tomorrow, not the God of yesterday. Theology and science must join hands and transform each other to bring beauty and healing to the Earth. We must be motivated by the power of love, not the love of power. The God of Tomorrow, the God who inspired past adventures of civilization and religion, is at work everywhere calling us beyond past doctrines and successes to greater and greater wholeness, to the apotheosis of beauty and love in the context of tragic history.

Whitehead and Teilhard believed that wherever truth, beauty, healing, and goodness are present, God is the source. Any action can be eucharistic and world building, no matter how small. Caring for children and grandchildren along with protesting climate change and developing vaccines manifest God's presence in the world. We can embrace the best of science along with the most inspirational religion to build the Earth of the Future.

Over fifty years ago, one of my theological mentors John Cobb asked, "Is it too late?" in reference to the environmental threats we face. Cobb believed that we needed a new theological vision to respond to our growing understanding of the environmental crisis, now articulated in terms of global climate change. Cobb did not guarantee success in responding to the environmental crisis, but he lived in hope for creative transformation in our economics, politics, and personal lives that would lead to healing the Earth. Indeed, the environmental movement of the 1970's led to the healing of the ozone layer, protecting species from extinction, and the return of clear skies over major metropolitan areas as first steps to healing the Earth. What we do in the micro and macro can cure or kill or repair or destroy. God calls with the vision of a beautiful future and we must respond with commitment and wisdom.

Teilhard lived in hope that the evolutionary process would lead to the Omega Point, the Christosphere, when the one and the many would be joined in Christ Consciousness. Perhaps, Teilhard was more hopeful for the human and planetary future, the divinization of the noosphere, than Cobb or Whitehead. But, Teilhard was well aware of the risks along the way to the Omega Point. There could be dead ends and obstacles, some accidental, but most resulting from humankind's failure to embrace a dynamic alternative to the individualism and violence of the present age. Despite the risks, the vision of Christ-Omega lends hope to our quest to heal the Earth.

Whitehead and Teilhard inspire the trinity of *vision, promise, and practice.* Their joint vision of a dynamic, interdependent, lively, value-laden and purposive universe, whose growth is called forth by creative and intelligent love, is something we can experience "within" the depths of our lives. God is the holiness in each thing and in us, and we can feel, if we pause and notice, God's passion and purpose moving within our lives. We can embrace the promise of creative union and complexity through visionary spiritual practices that unite us with all creation and the future that beckons us forward.

The powers of division and entropy are strong. The reptilian brain, promoted by the politics of fear and grievance, lures us to put greed and security, individual and national survival, ahead of compassion, empathy, and community. Yet, within the maelstrom of life, the loving arc of justice, compassion, creativity, and love lures us forward. The "fellow sufferer who understands" ignites a passion to heal the Earth and its Creatures so that Christ may be "all in all."

With hope for wholeness, unity, and joyful diversity, grounded in our partnership with the God of Tomorrow and Poet of the Universe, let us conclude with a prayer for the unfinished universe.

> *May the Energy of Love flow in and through you.*
> *May your hands radiate healing energy.*
> *May your heart beat with compassion.*
> *May your mind bring forth beautiful thoughts and words.*

May your spirit unite with Spirit to heal the Earth.
And may you claim your vocation in an unending adventure
Of companionship with God in creating
A universe where Love abounds, Thought excites,
Playfulness energizes, and Adventure inspires.
How can we keep from singing!
Amen.

BOOKS FOR THE ADVENTURE

Pierre Teilhard de Chardin, *Christianity and Evolution.* Translated by Rene Hague. New York: Harcourt Brace Jovanovich, 1969.

_____, *The Divine Milieu: An Essay on the Interior Life.* Translated by Bernard Wall. New York: Harper and Row, 1957.

_____, *The Future of Man.* Translated by Martin Denny. New York: Harper and Row, 1964.

_____, *Heart of Matter.* New York: Harcourt Brace Jovanovich, 1978.

_____, *Human Energy.* Translated by J.M. Cohen. New York: Harcourt Brace Jovanovich, 1969.

_____, *Hymn of the Universe.* Translated by Gerald Vann. New York: Harper and Row, 165.

_____, *Lettres a Jeanne Mortier.* Paris: Editions du Seuil, 1984.

_____, *The Phenomenon of Man (The Human Phenomenon.* Translated by Bernard Wall.

_____, *Science and Christ.* Translated by Rene Hague. New York: Harcourt Brace Jovanovich, 168.

_____, *Writings in Time of War.* Translated by Rene Hague. New York: Harper and Row, 1968.

Ilia Delio, *Birth of a Dancing Star: My Journey from Cradle Catholic to Cyborg Christian.* Maryknoll, NY: Orbis Books, 2019.

_____, *The Emergent Christ: Exploring the Meaning of Catholic in an Evolutionary Universe.* Maryknoll, NY: Orbis Books, 2011.

_____, *The Hours of the Universe: Reflections on God, Science, and the Human Journey* Maryknoll, NY: Orbis Books, 2021,

_____, *The Not-Yet God: Teilhard de Chardin, Carl Jung, and the Relational Whole*. Maryknoll, NY: Orbis Books, 2023.

_____, *The Unbearable Wholeness of God: God, Evolution, and the Power of Love*. Maryknoll, NY: Orbis Books, 2013.

Kathleen Duffy, *Teilhard's Mysticism: Seeing the Inner Face of Evolution*. Maryknoll, NY: Orbis Books, 2014.

_____, *Teilhard's Struggle: Embracing the Work of Evolution*. Maryknoll, NY: Orbis Books, 2019.

Bruce Epperly, *Homegrown Mystics: American Spiritual Visionaries*. Anamchara Books, 2024.

_____, *Jesus: Mystic, Healer, and Prophet*. Anamchara Books, 2023.

_____, *Mystics in Action: Twelve Saints for Today*. Maryknoll, NY: Orbis Books, 2020.

_____, *Process Theology: A Guide for the Perplexed*. London: Continuum, 2011.

_____, *Process Theology and Mysticism*. Gonzales, FL: _Energion, 2024.

_____, *Process Theology: Embracing Adventure with God*. Gonzales, FL: Energion, 2014.

_____, *The Mystic in You: Discovering a God-filled World*. Nashville: Upper Room Books, 2018.

_____, *We are All Mystics: How Spirituality Can Save Your Life and the World*, Anamchara Books, 2024.

Arthur Fabel and Donald St. John, editors. *Teilhard in the 21st Century; The Emerging Spirit of the Earth*. Maryknoll, NY: Orbis Books, 2003.

John Haught, *The Cosmic Vision of Teilhard de Chardin*. Maryknoll, NY: Orbis, 2021.

Ursula King, *Christ in All Things: Exploring Spirituality with Teilhard de Chardin*. Maryknoll, NY: Orbis Books, 2016.

_____, *Spirit of Fire: The Life and Vision of Pierre Teilhard de Chardin*. Maryknoll, NY: Orbis Books, 2014.

_____, *Teilhard de Chardin and Eastern Religions: Spiritu-
ality and Mysticism in an Evolutionary World*. Mahweh, NJ:
Paulist Press, 2011.

Victor Lowe, *Alfred North Whitehead: The Man and His Work*. Baltimore: Johns Hopkins Press, 1985.

Alfred North Whitehead. *Adventures of Ideas*. Paperback. New
York: The Free Press, 1933.

_____, *The Function of Reason*. Boston: Beacon Press, 1969.

_____, *Modes of Thought*. New York: The Free Press, 1968.

————. *Process and Reality: Corrected Edition*. Edited by David
Ray Griffin and Donald W. Sherburne. New York: The Free
Press, 1979.

_____, *Religion in the Making*. New York: Meridian, 1960.

_____, *Science and the Modern World*. New York: Free Press,
1967.

www.ingramcontent.com/pod-product-compliance
Lightning Source LLC
Chambersburg PA
CBHW031958080426
42735CB00007B/436